Finding My Pole Star

Memoir of an American hero's life
of faithful military service

James Lee Dozier

To learn more about this book and its author, please visit
GeneralDozier.com

Published by
Front Edge Publishing
42807 Ford Road, Suite 234
Canton, MI, 48187

Contents

I would like to dedicate this book to my first wife Judy,
and to my children Cheryl and Scott,
and to my second wife Sharlene,
as well as the soldiers with whom I was privileged to serve.
Sharlene and my children all encouraged me to write my life's story.

James Lee Dozier

Praise for
Finding My Pole Star

Finding My Pole Star is the amazing autobiography of Major General James Dozier, US Army (Ret), an individual dedicated throughout his life to the principles of strong leadership and service to God, to our great American nation, and to the military and his community.

The detailed accounts of challenges and successes are impressive in the messages which are delivered in support of active and creative leadership and trust in God. Credit is given in a humble manner to emphasize the support and guidance General Dozier received from his strong supportive family, his network of army and community leaders who served as mentors and advisors, as well as his enduring good friendships. General Dozier recognizes that these individuals, as well as his training at West Point, were the basis for his commitment to strong and effective leadership without which America and our constitutional democracy cannot continue as our beacon of freedom. This is a book for these times!

RADM A. Scott Logan, US Navy (Ret)

Conceived as an autobiography, *Finding My Pole Star* soon becomes a history book, where a wealth of personal experiences interlaces with American and international events.

When General Dozier was kidnapped, I was a young production assistant, on the staff with *NBC News Rome*. On duty practically day and night and under tremendous pressure, we had established the "Dozier Watch." Our eyes were glued to AP, ANSA and REUTERS wires, and the television and radio were turned on nonstop. Technology, in the early 80s, compared to today's, was rather primitive. We relied upon personal sources and contacts, verifying any possible rumor. One such tip in the middle of the night brought me and my cameraman to the middle of nowhere. It was a tiny village about a three-hour drive from Rome. Sadly, no trace of the general was found. When finally, he was rescued, the news was greeted with huge enthusiasm. In televised footage after the rescue on that January 28, 1982, our NBC crew is visible filming the Padua building where he was held, along with the crowd that had gathered.

Many years later General Dozier came to Italy for an interview with me and other meetings. On a sunny day we were walking in the center of Rome and he asked me where he could get a nice gift for Judy, his wife. We walked into a small store where he chose the gift and gave his credit card to the owner. The man read the general's name on the credit card and stood up. He said since thanks to the outcome of his kidnapping and that the Red Brigades finally were defeated, as a sign of gratitude, he would not accept any payment.

Finding My Pole Star is such a significant title. It is the expression of a lifetime search for the right path to follow, and yes, he indeed found his Pole Star in his military career, in his life as Judy's husband and Cheryl and Scott's father, and in his religious beliefs. He was able to cope with severe danger, threats, even the loss of Judy, but he always found the proper instruments with which to resurface. His having met Sharlene, after Judy had passed away, and then marrying this charming, generous, strong, fascinating lady is a gift from Above. It is a gift for me also. The Doziers mean so much to me, both individually and as a couple. They are blessed with the closeness of Pam and John Noland, now my friends, and the friends that all would like to have.

Dr. Raffaella Cortese de Bosis, Television Journalist and Author, RAI Italian State Television

Jim Dozier's life represents that of the consummate, vigorous American. Courageous, thoughtful, and determined in combat, capture and community, he adapted and won. Working with him as we led an Army Corps, or when he applied leadership techniques from the Center for Creative Leadership classroom to the harshness of captivity, he had the right stuff at the right time.

Lieutenant General Walter F. Ulmer, Jr., US Army (Ret), former President and CEO, Center for Creative Leadership

Then Colonel George Patton was the gold standard of combat leaders in Vietnam. My West Point classmate and life-long friend, Jim Dozier, was one of the big reasons Patton excelled as a regimental commander.

Jim dodged bullets beside Patton when they flew together, and at night, organized and briefed operational plans for the next day. Jim was and still is a dynamo of energy, who was at the top of his game in Vietnam. I still do not know when he got to sleep. Patton listened to Jim, acted on his advice, and treasured their relationship for the rest of his life. Rock solid integrity and common-sense advice, sprinkled with a sense of humor, define the superb soldier, who I have known and treasured for over 65 years.

Brigadier General John "Doc" Bahnsen, USA (Ret)

General Dozier had an outstanding military career, and later served his state and local community with true distinction. He was a member of and chaired several not-for-profit organizations that made a real difference in the lives of many. Often, he took over struggling groups and turned them into highly productive organizations. His strongest impact was in fostering both good government and education in the local school system, and in particular with the 15 high school Army JROTC programs in Lee County, Florida. General Dozier has been a powerful leader in the community and a role model to us all.

Gary L. Bryant, LTC, US Army (Ret)

General Dozier's story is told with the eye and voice of a man with wide and diverse experience, but also it is told most usefully in the salt-of-the earth voice of a man hewing as best he can to the truth of his own remembrance. His unselfconscious humility and his ability to tell an action packed and astonishingly detailed story make his book both fascinating and valuable for historians and everyday Americans alike. This is especially so for those of the 21st century generation.

General Dozier's story demonstrates that paying attention, while navigating our own lives through the individual sets of principles by which we live, helps clear our vision as to what our own Pole Star includes.

In my ten years of assisting young U.S. combat veterans from the 21st century Middle Eastern conflicts, I have learned from them the critical importance of their developing a personally important vision for their lives as they returned. Therefore, it is very important that the latest generation of Americans have the chance to hear this story. I recall one soldier telling me, "Dr. Chris, when we see someone of your generation, who has been on the brink of life-threatening situations, yet is now able to live a life with joy, it gives us hope that we can get there too." Jim Dozier's story, and especially the concrete and appealing way he tells it, offers that vision.

It is one thing to applaud our "heroes." It is another thing entirely to be one of those individuals who has developed a satisfying life of prosaic civilian tasks and responsibilities after risking his life, in service to his nation. Jim's story shows us the importance of each one of us in that effort.

Christine Wright-Isak, PhD, is a military sociologist and former business executive who teaches marketing at Florida Gulf Coast University's Lutgert College of Business. She is the founding faculty member of FGCU's "Students Who Served" organization and is an honorary member of the Lee Coast Chapter, Military Officers Association of America.

*The rule of virtue can be compared to the Pole
Star which commands the homage of the multitude
of stars without leaving its place.*

Confucius in *The Analects* (2:1)

Preface

I firmly believe that all of us who live on this earth are here to serve some purpose. God put us here for a reason. Many of us will never know what that purpose is. Others, like me, will get glimpses, from time to time, of our reason for being. To guide me as I moved down the road in my quest for a reason for being, I developed what I call a Pole Star. The North Star is a Pole Star. It is an unfailing beacon that provides direction. This is the story of how my Pole Star was developed over the years and how I used it to lead what I hoped would be a meaningful life of service to our great nation. In the various situations I encountered, my Pole Star was not always there like the North Star. My Pole Star developed over time, but fortunately for me, it developed at a pace that allowed me to meet some of my life's major challenges. It also was developed in increments, each one feeding on the one that preceded it. In retrospect, I was fortunate in that certain people and events provided direction for me at critical times.

As I put my life into perspective, it became apparent that there were numerous key drivers in my Pole Star development:

- My family.
- My friends while growing up.
- My religious upbringing.
- West Point.

- Military service and leadership lessons taught by two great commanders: MG George S. Patton III (Figure 1) and LTG Walter F. Ulmer (Figure 2, shown as an MG).
- Some superb southwest Florida physicians.
- Community and civilian business leaders with whom I became involved after I retired from military service.

Therefore, in the following chapters, I will focus on people and events that shaped the Pole Star of a small-town boy, who inadvertently followed a leadership career in military service that spanned 35 years. There also was a post-retirement leadership career of service in the civilian sector that has thus far spanned nearly another 35 years. Both have been fulfilling careers for me.

Fig. 1 MG George S. Patton

During my military career, I was a minor player in three major conflicts that helped the U.S. and our allies roll back the forces of communism in Europe, Korea, and Southeast Asia. It was my honor to have been able to provide leadership to a number of units and organizations that helped achieve those goals. During my post-retirement career, I was able to provide leadership to a number of community endeavors. This service, I believe, improved our local political processes and reinvigorated those not-for-profit organizations of which I am a member. For me, it proved that elements of my Pole Star were still guiding me.

Fig. 2 LTG Walter F. Ulmer

One lesson I learned very well was that enlightened leadership is absolutely essential to achieve a goal: LEADERSHIP IS EVERYTHING.

I will be ever thankful that God saw fit that I be a citizen of the United States of America. As I have travelled around the world, it has become more and more apparent that our great country is truly exceptional. The United States is now viewed as a beacon of freedom and opportunity for those in other parts of the planet who are less fortunate. In addition,

I thank God for the guidance my family, my comrades in arms and my friends provided as I developed my Pole Star and followed it. Certainly, God has allowed me to be a military and community leader who has touched the lives of many people. I hopefully have done so in a truly positive manner.

CHAPTER I

Ride of Terror and Beginnings

The Fiat hatchback made its way through the early evening, transporting me from Verona, Italy, to an unknown destination and to an equally unknown future. I was in the back, jammed into a steamer trunk, lying on my left side, knees to my chest, handcuffed with my hands behind my back. Each time I moved to make myself a little more comfortable, the handcuffs would tighten. Eventually, I would lose feeling in both of my hands. There were two other people in the car, one man and one woman. The man was driving. The woman was a passenger; I could smell her perfume. From time to time, the woman would check my breathing and pulse. In a strange way, that was reassuring.

About two hours earlier, I had answered the doorbell in our Verona, Italy apartment to let in two young men who had said they were plumbers. I had no idea that they were members of Italy's notorious Red Brigades. After a brief check of the apartment, looking for water leaks that they said were affecting the apartment beneath us, they showed their true intent by overpowering my wife and me. I was soon jammed into that steamer trunk and taken downstairs to the courtyard behind my apartment building. Soon I was to begin a ride to an unknown destination. Unknown to me at the time, my wife was uninjured, but left chained up in our apartment.

As I lay in the trunk, thinking about the preceding two hours and what the future might bring, my thoughts were running amok. I knew that I had been kidnapped, but I had no idea what lay ahead. However, during the struggle in my Verona apartment, I was able to glean several clues that indicated the kidnappers did not intend to kill me or my wife right away. Why I was kidnapped and what they would do with me were still mysteries at that point.

As I was growing up, I had read stories about individuals who had been kidnapped or held as prisoners of war. The story of *The Count of Monte Cristo* came to mind: one man's struggle to stay alive and free himself. I had had no training in how to deal with a situation like this. It was apparent that whatever situations were about to come my way, I had to deal with them, mostly relying on instinct and my military training. I asked God for guidance and hoped the traits of character that had been ingrained in me by my family and others would suffice. The ball was in my court. I was on my own.

Bound and terrified, I thought about my Pole Star, the guiding beacon that offered values for my life and helped lead me to a life of service. My path did not always follow a straight line, but with the guidance of parents, friends, mentors and my religious upbringing, I developed into the man I am.

Early Childhood

I was born in 1931 (Figure 1) and raised during the Great Depression in Arcadia, Florida, at the time a town of about 4,000 people. My sister, Joan, was born two years later. In that community there were a number of people who were influential in helping me develop my Pole Star. In many respects I was sort of a "free range" kid. My parents did not "ride herd" on me, but instead provided opportunities, though they did establish boundaries for my conduct, from which I sometimes strayed and was forced to deal with the consequences. Both of my parents were strong believers in experiential learning, the process of **learning** through experience, as well as "**learning** through reflection on doing."

Fig. 1 Baby Jim

Our father, Joseph Bythwood Dozier (Figure 2), was born in Greenville, Florida in 1887. After WWI and along with two brothers, they

established Doziers Incorporated, a
ladies and men's store in Arcadia that
sold shoes, clothes and dry goods.
My father became the secretary and
bookkeeper. Dad had served in WWI
(Figure 3) initially as a military policeman. He was assigned to the port
of Jacksonville, Florida, which was
a pretty rough place in those days.
He never talked much about his service, but one of his relatives told me
that being a military policeman in
Jacksonville was so rough that Dad
volunteered to go to France as a medic,
thus getting the nickname Doc. He

Fig. 2 Dad with Jim and Joan

was gassed in France, which no doubt
affected his overall health in later years.
He brought home from the war a number
of souvenirs, which I still have and cher-
ish: a WWI American GI steel helmet, a
German bayonet, a Prussian leather helmet
with a spear-tip ornament on top, German
bread made mainly of sawdust and a 9 mm
long-barreled Luger, complete with holster
and detachable stock. Probably because
of the gassing, he died young at age 57 in
1945, shortly after V-E Day in Europe.

Our mother, Leota Caruthers, was
born in 1900, along with a twin sister (not
identical), Lena, in Alpine, Texas (Figure
4). Since their mother had died during
childbirth, they were raised by an aunt
who brought them to Tampa, Florida. Our
mother was a small (5' even), very athletic
woman.

Fig. 3 Jim's father in
WWI uniform

Mother attended Florida State College for Women (FSCW), now Florida State University (FSU) (Figure 5). She graduated with a degree in education, taught for a while in Quincy, Florida, then got a teaching job in Arcadia where she met our father. While at FSCW, she participated in track and field events: the hurdles, the javelin; and archery. She was also a member of the Kappa Delta Sorority. She taught for 35 years in the Arcadia schools and was known as a strict disciplinarian, but a wonderful teacher.

Fig. 4 Leota and Lena

School Years

The house (Figure 6) I grew up in was across the street from the playground of West Elementary School, one of two elementary schools in Arcadia. West Elementary, a building housing the cafeteria/gymnasium and also DeSoto County High School, all occupied a single block. My sister and I were thus able to walk to school, as did most of the students who lived in Arcadia proper. The school bus system was designed to service those who lived "in the country," too far from Arcadia to walk.

Fig. 5 Leota Dozier

Most of the friends we had growing up were those who lived in Arcadia proper and in the nearby Baptist orphanage. My parents and my sister and I all attended Sunday school and church on Sundays. Our community was evenly split between

Fig. 6 Boyhood home, now circa 2010

Baptists, Methodists and Presbyterians, and we also had a few Catholic and Jewish friends. Our family interacted with friends from each of the faith groups.

Several years ago, I learned that my father in the family business was a very meticulous bookkeeper. Howard Melton, one of my mother's former students, but then the president of the DeSoto County Historical Society, approached me at a DeSoto County church picnic. He asked: "Jimmy, can you keep a secret?" I told him, "No, Howard, I cannot keep a secret." He said that I had to because he had just been given my father's business ledgers for the DeSoto County Historical Society Museum and that they were controversial. He instead wanted me to keep them so he would not have to display the documents.

It turns out that if the accounts (most people charged items in those depression days) were current, Dad kept the records in black ink. If they were delinquent, he noted that in red ink. Howard's concern was that some of DeSoto County's more notable individuals during the depression accrued a lot of red ink and their descendants might be embarrassed. I told him that "bad news doesn't get any better with age," but I would gladly take them off his hands. Several years later, after Howard had died, his successor learned about the ledgers and said that she was not worried about family concerns. They are now displayed in the society museum.

Dad was a slender, very courteous man who enjoyed gardening, hunting and fishing. When hunting doves, shooting them on the wing with a shotgun, he would use me as his bird-dog retriever. He would shoot them and I would run out and pick them up. We had the same arrangement when he and his brothers would shoot fish in the nearby tidal creeks. When pods of mullet, a salt water fish, would swim under a bridge, they would fire their high powered, former military rifles into the pods, thus stunning some of the fish. My job was to go into the water with a dip net and retrieve the stunned fish. Since most of the "mullet runs" occurred when the weather was chilly, this was not at all that enjoyable.

When I was 6 years old, Dad gave me a Remington pump .22-caliber rifle (Figure 7). After a flock of doves had passed and I had picked up the ones he had shot, I was allowed to shoot those who settled in nearby trees until the next flock arrived. He taught me to be very meticulous with how I used and maintained the rifle. In fact, it was my job to clean all the rifles and shotguns after they had been used. As a result, I became a "good shot," as well as gained a healthy respect for various firearms. From time to time, I would also work in the family store, sweeping up after closing, as well as at times clerking in the men's department during the Saturday rush.

During WWII, Dad religiously followed the news. H. V. Kaltenborn and Walter Winchell were his favorite newsmen, and the evening radio news (television was yet to come) was an essential part of his day. I also listened and became interested in the names and places talked about on the radio and printed in the newspapers. As a result, I probably learned more world geography from events in WWII than I did in school.

Fig. 7 Jim with new .22-cal. rifle

My father was also a strong believer in the importance of our country's strength with regard to our leadership on the world stage. On many occasions he commented about how our efforts in WWI and WWII turned the tide. During WWII, he was a cheerleader for our actions both in Europe and the Pacific.

My closest friends were Ray Cassells, Dan Ralls, David Dishong, the Dykes boys (Louis and Walter) and George Birk (later to become my stepbrother). We all did reasonably well in school and participated in most school activities. Most of us were not really challenged by the curriculum in those days, so we had plenty of time for other activities in and out of school.

Ray and I were in the school band and played basketball. Dan was bigger than the rest of us, so he was on the football team. George eventually went away to military school. Since we played trumpets in the high school band, Ray and I were called upon from time to time to play taps at military funerals for veterans and those killed in WWI and WWII, with most buried in local cemeteries.

Growing up in Arcadia was like growing up in an extended family. All of our parents were involved with each other's children. If we misbehaved, usually our parents knew about it before we got home. Since my mother was a teacher, I had a disciplinary disadvantage.

Discipline in Desoto County public schools was pretty rigorous. The principals and coaches were the enforcers: all were no-nonsense disciplinarians who had no compunctions about using the "board of education." Our high school principal would sometimes give us a choice of so many licks by the board of education, or copy pages in the dictionary. If we were in a hurry to get home after school (most of us had after-school jobs), we took the licks. The coaches administered the licks as they saw fit.

Since Arcadia was a relatively small town, sometimes letting an incident run its course was the best disciplinary action. For instance, shortly after WWII, one of our neighbors, Mrs. Elinor Morgan, built an in-ground swimming pool. It proved to be a magnet for kids in the neighborhood, myself included. George Birk, who lived across the street from Mrs. Morgan, would notify us when she left her home. We would then rush to get into our bathing suits and get in the pool. Since there were no secrets in a town like Arcadia, Mrs. Morgan, of course, knew all about us. She told our parents that she would put a fence around the pool to see if that would solve the problem. *It did not.*

Since the fence didn't solve the issue, one of her neighbors who was involved with agriculture, suggested that she should put a flock of geese inside the pool fence. He told her that was the way distilleries in Scotland provided early warning of intruders. The neighbor said that geese are very territorial. In addition to being very noisy, they would usually attack intruders. That is exactly what happened.

We had learned how to get over the fence, but the geese were a problem we had not counted on. When we climbed over the fence, the geese became very noisy, and as we tried to get into the pool, they attacked us by beating us with their wings and pecking our feet. Soon a couple of us lost toenails. That ended our forays into Mrs. Morgan's pool.

During WWII in elementary and junior high school, we played war games with each other, using wooden guns we made ourselves. Usually it was Ray, Dan, George and I on one side and the Dykes boys and their friends on the other. We established our own ground rules for our engagements and became quite good at tactics and deception, as well as cover and concealment.

As we got a little older, we spent less time with war games and more time hunting and fishing. We hunted squirrels and rabbits in the Peace River swamps, about a mile from town. All of us had .22-caliber rifles that our parents allowed us to use as we saw fit.

We also made fishing spears out of the arrows my mother had used in college. My mother had several longbows and an assortment of arrows which she turned over to us. In addition, we made our own underwater spear-fishing gear. We used door springs encased in iron pipe on either side of an iron pipe barrel to propel our spears.

We became pretty handy with basic hand tools, mostly provided by our fathers. When he turned 16, Dan Ralls was allowed to drive a 1936 Chevy coupe that had been in his family for years. That opened up new spear-fishing vistas for us. We were now able to drive to lucrative spear-fishing spots along the nearby Gulf of Mexico.

From junior high on, all of us had jobs. Dan and I delivered the afternoon *Tampa Daily Times* newspaper and Ray worked in a drug store. We also designed, built and flew model airplanes. We spent a lot of time with Lionel model trains.

My great-aunt (Grandmere) (Figure 8), who had raised Mother in Tampa, lived with us in Arcadia until she died in 1940. Since Mother was always involved in outside activities, Grandmere and a Black woman named Mary Jones did most of the cooking and child-raising.

Both ladies were pretty authoritarian and had no qualms about corporal punishment. This usually involved a switch that we were personally required to pick from a tree in the yard. Mary Jones was treated as a member of our household. When we went to a beach during the summer, usually Siesta Key, near Sarasota, or Anna Maria, near Bradenton, Mary would go with us. Joan and I often would play on one of the beaches with our dog.

While we swam and frolicked on the beach (Figure 9) and in the surf, Mary (Figure 10) loved to fish. One

Fig. 8 Grandmere with Joan

Fig. 9 Jim and Joan on the Beach

summer at Anna Maria, while fishing from the town pier, she hooked a huge nurse shark, a rather docile, but still a large fish. We were all startled by her cries of "hep me please, hep me please!"

Fig. 10 Mary Jones with Jim and Joan

Everyone on the pier rushed over to help her land the fish, but alas, the shark was so heavy that her light fishing tackle would not allow her to get it out of the water and up onto the pier. We finally cut the line and let the fish go. From that point on, Mary was a welcome fixture in the pier-fishing community.

My mother was a tough teacher in the DeSoto County (Arcadia) public schools for nearly 35 years. Even today, when I visit Arcadia, her former students often tell me what a positive influence she was on their lives. She certainly was on ours. She believed that all of us were capable of more than we were demonstrating, so she ever so gently and subtly, but also continuously pushed us toward our limits. Our parents brought out a competitive, independent nature in both my sister and me. For instance, I was encouraged to join the high school boxing and basketball teams. Mother made both my sister, Joan, and me take piano and tap dance lessons. When I was having some trouble with high school math, she arranged for a tutor. As previously mentioned, she was also a firm believer in experiential learning.

In the summer of 1947, my mother made it possible for my future stepbrother and me to go to the Dominican Republic and work on a ranch run by my future stepfather, George Birk. That cured me of ever wanting to be a cowboy! George had previously moved his family from the Dominican Republic to Arcadia for safety just prior to WWII. They became our backdoor neighbors and good friends. In order to develop my self-confidence and self-sufficiency, my mother arranged with relatives during my early teens (she put me on trains alone and relatives met me when I arrived), for me to travel coast to coast twice by myself. In previous years, I was sent to summer camps on my own for the same reasons.

My mother always made sure that I had summer jobs, but I had to seek them out myself with her subtle urging. I was not provided an allowance. As a result, I had an after-school bicycle paper route that earned me enough money to self-finance some of my hobbies, such as model airplanes and trains. My prime responsibility at home was to take care of our yard. I also did yard work for her friends. Mother involved us in religious activities early on. She made a special effort to acquaint us with the diversity of our planet's great and major religions. One of the religious books she made us read was *Fire Upon the Earth*. It gave a history of and discussed the highlights of the Earth's major religions.

In Summary, Here Are the Major Influences on My Early Life:

My father, who taught me respect for honesty, firearms, hard work, independence, and the virtue of "gofer" type tasks, such as being a bird dog. He also instilled in me a sense of patriotism and a feeling for "American exceptionalism."

My mother taught me other life skills such as competitiveness, self-confidence, self-sufficiency, the importance of a good education, the virtues of being a part of a community, as well as developing my religious outlook. More on the importance of religion to me in a later chapter.

My family and friends provided a firm basis for the development of my Pole Star.

CHAPTER 2

Road to West Point

I would like to say that a military career was something that I had longed to pursue—a career goal. However, I cannot say that. Instead, it was the result of many fits and starts after graduating from high school.

I graduated from DeSoto County High School in 1949. There were only 38 students in my graduating class. My mother decided that I would best benefit from going to a small junior college before throwing me to the wolves at a large university. It made sense. Several of her students had benefited from this process. So, based largely on feedback from prior students, she enrolled me in Mars Hill Junior College, a predominantly Baptist school in Mars Hill, North Carolina. I did not live in a dormitory, but in a small house on campus that housed maybe a dozen or so students.

I roomed with a WWII veteran, Ed Dowdy, who was dedicated to hard work and studying. He was a good influence. I made pretty good grades and found that I had an aptitude for chemistry. Ed was in his late 20s, came from a rather poor family in Virginia, and was taking advantage of the WWII GI Bill. I forget what he was majoring in, perhaps religious studies, as many students at Mars Hill were doing in those days. Ed was taking advantage of an opportunity that had eluded others in his family. As a result, we developed a rather rigid, no nonsense study routine. As previously mentioned, there were about a dozen other students who lived in the same house, but they weren't as dedicated to study as were the two of us. I think Ed was so focused, not only because of his meager upbringing, but also and primarily because of his military service. He definitely had a decided and most positive influence on me. He, of course, would tell me stories of his military service. This no doubt influenced my decision, at least to some extent, to enlist in the Florida National Guard the next summer.

For cost of living reasons, about midway through the year at Mars Hill, I moved from the dormitory house on campus to a private residence just across the street from the campus. It was owned by Mrs. Beulah Bowden, who rented several rooms to students. I shared a room with Latimer Farr, from Wauchula, Florida. It was a mutually good arrangement in that Latimer was diligent with his studies. In addition, Mrs. Bowden did not put up with any horseplay, as sometimes happened in the previous building.

Latimer later became a very successful lawyer in his hometown of Wauchula.

Our chemistry professor, Mr. Vernon Wood, was a semi-invalid who lectured from a wheelchair. He was a delightful person who had a great sense of humor, thus making a complex subject enjoyable. Mr. Wood was a down-to-earth person who related chemical reactions to real life issues, such as why salt and sugar were used both in seasoning and the preservation of foods. He made a somewhat dry subject come alive. I was also active in intramural sports: basketball, football and tennis. When I enrolled at Mars Hill, I had no clear career goals. On the advice of one of my mother's former students who had attended Mars Hill, I enrolled in the general science curriculum. I had enjoyed chemistry in high school and fortunately chemistry was required in the general science curriculum.

After a year at Mars Hill, my mother and I decided that I was ready for the University of Florida. That turned out to be a premature judgment. During the summer between leaving Mars Hill and entering the University of Florida, I, along with some of my high school classmates, joined the local Army National Guard unit. Battery D, 712th AAA, was a 90 mm gun anti-aircraft artillery unit (Figure 1).

Although I did not know it at the time, this turned out to be one of the most important, life-changing decisions I would make. Quite frankly, I joined the National Guard because it was the social thing to do. Most

Fig. 1 National Guard Unit 1950

of my friends were already members. I was sworn into the guard on June 1, 1950. The North Koreans invaded South Korea about three weeks later. During the summer of 1950, we departed for Fort Stewart, Georgia for our annual two weeks of summer training. Fort Stewart was a National Guard training center at that time. It would later become a permanent post and the home of a Regular Army mechanized division.

In 1950, the only permanent (brick) building at Fort Stewart was the telephone exchange. There were a number of wooden structures on the post, but National Guard units lived in tents during summer training. I was assigned to the fire direction platoon, which consisted of a van-mounted radar set and antenna, and a trailer-mounted fire direction computer.

The radar tracked the targets, then fed target data through an old analog computer, which told the guns where to point. Our platoon sergeant was Buddy Woodley, who was several years older than me, but whom I had known all of my life. Our families were close friends. After our two weeks at Fort Stewart, where we conducted live fire drills, we returned to Arcadia and our regular summer activities. I then made preparations to enroll at the University of Florida in Gainesville.

At first, I did not do very well at Florida and I changed my major from chemical engineering to agricultural engineering, mainly because it was an easier course. Phi Kappa Tau fraternity had by that time beckoned. I became very involved in its activities and as a result my grades began to suffer. They suffered to the extent that they were never high enough for me to become a brother in the fraternity. Thus, to this day I remain a Phi Kappa Tau pledge.

Since the University of Florida was a land grant university, many members of the fraternity were in the Army Reserve Officer Training Corps (ROTC), as was I. Since I already had a summer of National Guard training at Fort Stewart under my belt, the ROTC drills came easy.

Before the end of my first year at Florida, rumors began to circulate that our guard unit was to be federalized. The rumors turned out to be true, so on May 1, 1951, our entire battalion was federalized and sent back to Fort Stewart for mobilization training. Thus, I never finished my year at the University of Florida. I was probably saved from flunking several courses.

Once our unit was at Fort Stewart, a number of our hometown officers and enlisted non-commissioned officers (NCOs) were sent off for additional training and were replaced by Regular Army officers and NCOs.

D Battery was initially composed of most of the military-age males in the Arcadia area, few of whom had any prior military experience. We were true citizen soldiers. For instance, our battery commander was our mailman, our maintenance sergeant was a mechanic at the local Ford garage, our first sergeant had prior military experience, but was working as a full-time employee of the Florida National Guard. No one was drafted in DeSoto County for nearly two years after we were federalized. All of our training before then was focused on individual skills and battery level training. We had never trained as a battalion. An anti-aircraft artillery battalion at that time consisted of four firing batteries (A, B, C, and D), plus a headquarters (HQ) battery.

Our battery was located in Arcadia, another was located in Fort Myers (40 miles away), another at Avon Park (50 miles away), and another and our battalion HQ were located in Miami (150 miles away). The only time we encountered the other battalion units was during the two weeks of summer training at Fort Stewart, where we concentrated on firing our weapons. By no stretch of the imagination were we prepared to perform a wartime mission. As happens after most wars, the military goes through a period of neglect. This was certainly true for our National Guard unit. The name of the game once we were federalized was to get the battalion ready for combat as soon as possible. That meant replacing the key leaders with already trained personnel, while "hometown" key leaders were sent to Army schools for training. Some of the hometown key leaders eventually returned to the unit, but most became individual replacements for other units.

It did not take long for some of us to realize that the unit was in pretty bad shape and would take a long time to be combat ready. Since we were committed to two years of active duty and had no clue as to how long the Korean War would last, most of us thought it better to serve in some other organization. We started looking for various ways to leave the unit.

Our newly assigned battery commander was a Regular Army captain named Johnson, a real professional. Upon taking command, he made it a point to visit each section of the battery for a briefing regarding how the battery members did their jobs. His aim was obviously to find out how well we knew our skills. I later used this technique when I became a commander of a new unit.

I was assigned to brief him on the fire control computer, a key part of our fire direction section, which included a truck-mounted radar. I had studied the inter-relationships of the entire fire direction system, so my briefing was rather comprehensive. I guess I impressed Captain Johnson because he later called me to his office to discuss the possibility of attending several Army schools, including OCS. I applied for several, including volunteering for duty in Korea.

While this process was maturing, Captain Johnson called several of us to his office to tell us that the civil service designating exams for the service academies were to be given at the Fort Stewart Education Center the next week. He encouraged us to take them. Several members of the unit, including me, took them with three of us qualifying for the United States Military Academy (West Point) Prep School (USMAPS) at Stewart Air Force Base (AFB), Newburgh, New York. At the end of August 1951, we three headed north to the prep school. Our National Guard unit also headed north later to Sandy Hook, New Jersey, with the mission to protect the New York City area from air attack.

I learned a very important leadership lesson from Captain Johnson: When one recognizes untapped abilities in a subordinate, encourage that person to extend his/her horizons.

Admission to a service academy is a two-step process: nomination and appointment. An applicant must first be nominated and these nominations come from various sources. Members of the United States House and Senate are the traditional sources, but each branch of the armed forces plus the president, vice president and several others may also nominate. For instance, the son or daughter of a Congressional Medal of Honor recipient is eligible for a nomination. In most cases all nominations, except those from the House and Senate, are competitive. The service academies then screen those nominated and extend appointments.

USMAPS on Stewart AFB was located just north of the academy itself, and it was a life changer for me. The whole atmosphere was competitive and I thrived on it. I found that each of us with National Guard nominations was competing with two others for an appointment to West Point.

Even our class assignments were competitive. After each grading session, we were reassigned to sections based upon our grades, mirroring the grading system at West Point. The higher sections were composed of students with better grades. The lower sections were composed of those who needed more help. I was able to stay in the higher sections, so I had more free time than those needing help. Even where we sat in class was based upon grades; the higher grades sat in the rear of the class.

The living conditions at the prep school were far better than those at Fort Stewart, Georgia, where we lived in tents with dirt floors. At the prep school, we had brick barracks with hardwood floors. We were required to pull kitchen police (KP) duty, but that was itself a learning exercise. One day while on KP, a couple of us became upset with Tex, an old Army mess sergeant. He had been hard on us for some minor infraction earlier in the day, so we decided to get even. While peeling potatoes in a mechanical peeler that spun the potatoes against the abrasive sides of the machine, we reduced them to marble size. Tex let us have it and told us to never test him again. He put us to work peeling another batch of potatoes—by hand!

Ryans 901 Club, Newburgh, New York

Newburgh was the nearest town to Stewart AFB. Since there was not much to do on base during weekends, most of us headed to downtown

Newburgh. We would usually go to a fast-food restaurant for a quick dinner and then head to a bar named Ryans 901 Club, which seemed to cater to those stationed at Stewart AFB. One of the Saturday night regulars was the detective story author Mickey Spillane. He would regale us with stories of how he researched his novels.

Most of us at the prep school had received competitive nominations to West Point, rather than by the more secure congressional nominations. Competitive nominations were just what the name implies. It usually meant that you were competing with at least two other applicants for an appointment. A congressional nomination usually meant a guaranteed appointment to the service academy, as long as the appointee was otherwise qualified. As a result, those with competitive nominations went back and forth to Washington to prowl the halls of Congress looking for a congressman who had not filled all of his/her nomination vacancies. These applicants were mostly unsuccessful in their quests.

I successfully competed for a National Guard appointment and entered the United States Military Academy at West Point in early July 1952 as a member of the Class of 1956. Having had prior military service and the opportunity to attend the West Point prep school, the rigors of Beast Barracks and Fourth-Class year (Plebe year) were not particularly troublesome for me. I knew what to expect with regard to hazing, and the prep school had thoroughly prepared me for the first year at the academy. In addition, the prep school academics prepared us almost completely for first year academics at West Point. Also, much of the material covered was a repeat of what I had studied at the University of Florida: calculus, effective writing, physics, etc. In addition, that prior competitive, regimented atmosphere more than adequately prepared us for the rigors of Plebe year.

United States Military Academy West Point, New York

I did not realize it at the time, but West Point, in addition to my parents, would provide the key basic values incorporated in my Pole Star. I swore the following oath when I entered West Point:

> *I, James Lee Dozier, do solemnly swear that I will support the Constitution of the United States and bear true allegiance to the National Government; that I will maintain and defend*

*the sovereignty of the United States paramount to any and all
allegiance, sovereignty, or fealty I may owe to any state, county
or country whatsoever; and that at all times obey the legal orders
of my superior officers and the rules and articles governing the
armies of the United States.*

West Point marked an important turning point in the development
of my Pole Star. The values of "Duty, Honor, Country" inculcated at the
academy influenced me for the rest of my life, and I discovered that I
thrived on being part of a structured, competitive military environment.
The West Point Honor System was particularly influential: "A cadet will
not lie, cheat or steal, or tolerate those who do." In practical terms, we
were taught that our word was our bond, and that if we said something, it
was true to the best of our knowledge. The Cadet Prayer was also influential. Both the Honor System and the Cadet Prayer contain thoughts that
provide pretty darn good guidelines for living a meaningful life.

Cadet Prayer

*O God, our Father, Thou Searcher of Men's Hearts, help us draw
near to Thee in sincerity and truth. May our religion be filled
with gladness and our worship of Thee be natural. Strengthen
and increase our admiration for honest dealing and clean
thinking, and suffer not our hatred of hypocrisy and pretense
ever to diminish. Encourage us in our endeavor to live above
the common level of life. Make us to choose the harder right
instead of the easier wrong, and never to be content with a half-
truth when the whole can be won. Endow us with courage that
is born of loyalty to all that is noble and worthy, that scorns to
compromise with vice and injustice and knows no fear when
truth and right are in jeopardy. Guard us against flippancy
and irreverence in the sacred things of life. Grant us new ties of
friendship and new opportunities of service. Kindle our hearts
in fellowship with those of a cheerful countenance, and soften
our hearts with sympathy for those who sorrow and suffer. Help
us maintain the honor of the Corps untarnished and unsullied
and to show forth in our lives the ideals of West Point in doing*

our duty to Thee and to our country. All of which we ask in the
name of the Great Friend and Master of Men. Amen.

With the guidelines provided by the Honor System and the Cadet
Prayer, we launched into a very rigorous four-year program that thoroughly prepared us to be officers and leaders in our nation's armed forces.

A very important trait learned at West Point was time and resource
management. Plebe year in particular was designed to be stressful from
a time management standpoint. There was seldom enough time for an
unstructured cadet to successfully complete all of the tasks assigned. Successful cadets quickly learned to prioritize and devote sufficient time to
those tasks that were most important. In later years, this was an attribute
that proved to be extremely valuable when in combat or when commanding a unit.

All cadets followed
the same rigorous
physical training pro-
gram—we all were given
classes in boxing and
wrestling. Our swim-
ming ability was tested
and we were encouraged
to become involved with
varsity and intramural
team sports. Boxing
came naturally to me, in
that I had been on the

Fig. 2 Four cadets

boxing team in high school. I played halfback on our company intramural football team. I also participated in intramural tennis, squash and
track events as a member of our company 440 and 880 relay team.

In Figure 2, I am the cadet on the right in athletic gear. A valuable
sports lesson I learned as a cadet came from my tennis and squash coach
Leif Nordlie, a no-nonsense Norwegian American. He drilled into us
that there are only two ways to win at either squash or tennis: "You
either learn to play your opponent's game better than he does, or force
your opponent to play your game." Leif also added, "Once you get your
opponent down, never let him up." His advice was a great lesson in both

tactics and strategy. I have applied that lesson countless times since, in both my military and civilian careers.

Unlike upperclassmen, during the first year at West Point, Plebes were not allowed to leave West Point for any reason, including holidays like Thanksgiving and Christmas. However, during my Plebe year, an opportunity arose that allowed a number of Plebes to travel a bit. The West Point Protestant chapel choir had been depleted by the previous year's graduation and cheating scandal. Marty Mayer, the chapel organist and choirmaster persuaded the authorities to open up the choir to Plebes. I, and several others in my company, took advantage of that opportunity and successfully auditioned for the choir. We made several trips to New York City and surrounding areas, which provided a welcome relief from the rigors of Plebe year. However, my time with the choir ended the next year when we were required to audition again. This time I didn't make the cut. I now tell folks that I got kicked out of the West Point chapel choir, which was true!

During my time at West Point, all cadets took the same courses. I found that I was pretty good at math and the sciences, but was weak in languages and English, even though my mother had been an English teacher. Roughly 14–15 cadets were assigned to each classroom or "section," as in the prep school. We were graded daily in each class and periodically reassigned to a new section based on our grades. It was a good system and allowed the professors to tailor their instruction to the abilities of the students. I was assigned to Company I, First Regiment (Company I-1) and remained assigned there for the next four years. Those in my class in that company formed a very close bond and we have remained in close contact ever since (Figure 3). Bob Caron, standing

Fig. 3 Cadet friends

on the right in the photo, flew the last helicopter from the roof of the U.S. Embassy in Saigon, as we vacated Vietnam in the wake of the North Vietnamese invasion.

After Plebe year and summer leave, we Third Classmen (sophomores) were now called Yearlings as we returned to West Point for summer training at nearby Camp Buckner. It was, in essence, two months devoted to military basic training. At Camp Buckner we learned basic soldiering: leadership, marksmanship, personal hygiene, map reading, etc. I was assigned as the S-3 (training and operations officer) on the cadet battalion staff and as such I helped plan and organize much of the training. It was a good experience that would stand me in good stead later in my career.

Fig. 4 Yearling Jim Dozier

During our Yearling year (Figure 4), we were allowed more latitude with regard to picking our roommates. Roommates originally were assigned by our company tactical officer during Plebe year. Two friends, with whom I developed a close relationship, were Walt Sager and Bill Westcott, both of whom I had known in prep school. Both also had prior enlisted service. We were older than most of our class and we were frequently turned to for advice by some of our younger classmates. Bill Westcott's family lived in nearby northern New Jersey. His home and family became a second home and family to many of us. We would often congregate there when we had a free weekend away from the academy. Walt Sager was from California. Although the three of us were from different parts of the United States and had different backgrounds, we became and remained close friends.

After Yearling year, we were called Second Classmen (juniors) or Cows. During Cow summer our class was flown around the United States on military aircraft, visiting bases of our sister services. It was time well spent. It gave us an appreciation of the dynamics of the other military services we would operate with in later years. When Cow academic year began, I was appointed as a "Cow corporal" and a position in our company chain of command as a squad leader. It was my first military leadership position. Even though there were several upperclassmen in the squad, my primary responsibilities revolved around developing the Plebes that were assigned to us.

I relished the challenge. The appointment as a Cow corporal was the first indication I had that my superiors, in this case our company tactical officer Major Hank Hughes, considered me to have potential for leadership. However, such recognition had its drawbacks: During this period Major Hughes assigned several classmates who were lacking in military aptitude as my roommates, hoping that they would learn and develop by association. It didn't work very well and none of them improved. Some cadets were just not adaptable to military life and should have been eliminated much earlier.

During summer leave between Cow and Firstie (senior) year, two classmates, Mario Nicolais, Nick Bruno and I hitchhiked to Europe by military air. We caught a flight from Westover AFB, Massachusetts, to Frankfurt, Germany, via the Azores. From Frankfurt, we traveled by train to Naples, Italy. The year was 1954, just nine years after the end of WWII. During that train ride, I got my first inkling of the appreciation that Europeans had for the sacrifices Americans made on their behalf during WWII. It also was my first real insight into the destruction that occurred during the war.

At a stop in northern Italy during that train ride, two Italian carpenters were assigned seats in our compartment. Both had been WWII prisoners of war (POWs), held for several years in a POW camp in Texas. Since we were traveling in our khaki uniforms, they immediately recognized us as Americans. They both spoke a little English, and with the help of Mario's translations, they began to thank us for what we had done for Italy during those tragic years.

They related how they had worked in a military commissary in Texas and had been fed real butter and other rationed items in the POW camp, while Americans who shopped in the commissary were still subject to wartime rationing. Both men had relatives in the United States. They went on to say that they had tried several times to escape, so they would not be sent back to Italy, but each time they were caught. During subsequent trips to Europe, I would hear similar stories from others who lived through WWII— heartfelt appreciation for sacrifices Americans had made for Europeans during the war.

After an overnight stay in Rome, we caught another train to Naples where we were met by Mario's Italian relatives.

Fig. 5 Nick and Mario in Calitri

We then drove by car up into the hills north of Naples to the little town of Calitri. We were warmly welcomed and wined and dined (Figure 5). In those days, there was a significant communist element in Italy, including Calitri, so we were advised to wear civilian clothes rather than our uniforms. Late each evening before dinner, we

Fig. 6 Jim and Nick in St. Peter's Square

would meet friends of Mario's relatives in the small town square where we were peppered with questions regarding life in the United States. We also were thanked for our help in liberating them from fascist and Nazi rule during the war.

After almost a week of endless eating, Nick Bruno and I decided we needed a break. We left Mario with his relatives in Calitri and caught an embassy courier plane (a Grumman Avenger) in Naples and flew to Rome (Figure 6). Mario joined us several days later. After touring Rome and Pompeii, we then took a train back to Frankfurt and caught a military flight back to the United States.

When we returned to West Point later that summer, I was assigned as a Cadet Company Commander for summer training of Third Classmen at Camp Buckner. Also, that summer I commanded a cadet company that participated in the inauguration ceremonies for the new United States Air Force Academy (USAFA), held at Lowry AFB in Colorado.

Lowry was the first home of the USAFA while the campus at Colorado Springs was under construction.

Further Religious Development

When our Firstie academic year began, I was again assigned as an S-3, this time on our cadet 3rd Battalion, 1st Regiment staff (Figure 7) and reunited with Walt Sager and Bill Westcott as roommates. During the previous summer, Walt and Bill, both Protestants, had become engaged to Catholic girls and so had to undergo conversion training to be Catholics. These classes were held at the cadet Catholic Chapel. In our room after each of their training sessions, we would have many serious discussions, often about religion in general, as well as differences between the Catholic and Protestant faiths more specifically. Though I had grown up in the very religious environment of the Methodist Church, I had not developed any serious religious beliefs.

Fig 7. 3rd Battalion, 1st Regiment staff

As a result of our discussions, I developed reservations with some of the tenets of Catholicism such as intercession, confession to a priest, true faith and praying to a saint. These discussions also made me question some of the tenets of Protestantism. For instance, both religions are very hierarchical, talking about kings, obedience, admission of sins, etc. The more Walt, Bill and I talked, the more I questioned the importance of organized religion, but I never questioned the concept of God and prayer.

My reasoning developed as follows: There is a tremendous amount of order in our known universe. It is hard for me, as an engineer, to believe that this meticulous order was created by happenstance. There had to be some force that created such an orderly universe, one that allowed human beings to evolve and become a part of that order. For want of a name, I call that force God. Thus, it stands to reason that human beings are here for some purpose. Compared to other living things, due mainly to our ability to reason, humans are currently at the top of the evolutionary pecking order on our planet. So, as a human, and perhaps being a little conceited, I believe I am here as part of God's plan for me, and by extension, I feel that I have a special relationship with God.

As a result of the above reasoning, when I pray, I simply ask God for guidance. I believe I have the ability to make decisions that are in sync with God's plan. For the issues that I cannot control, I pray for understanding. Probably, most of us will never completely understand God's plan for us, but from time to time, we will get glimpses. The above can be summed up by advice from a wise friend in Fort Myers, Florida, whose mantra was: "Play the hand you were dealt to the absolute best of your ability, then depend on God to govern the outcome."

Walt and Bill converted to Catholicism, married their girlfriends and became parents of successful children. Walt and his wife, Elaine, have now passed away. Bill and his wife, Doris, live in the North Carolina mountains.

Judy

During the summer of 1955, before Firstie year, I met Judith Irene Stimpson while on a class trip to Fort Belvoir, Virginia. She was a delightful young lady who was born and raised in Washington, D.C. Judy was a member of Pi Beta Phi sorority at George Washington University. She also had a part-time clerical job with the FBI. During those days, the cadets from the service academies were sometimes in the district for various reasons, such as parades or class trips. On these occasions, an organized group of "hosts" would invite cadets into their homes for cookouts or picnics.

The hosts would also invite members of local university sororities, usually on a one-for-one basis, according to the number of cadets. The garden party cookout (hamburgers, beer and soft drinks) where I met Judy was in the backyard of a State Department officer. We happened to meet as we sat down to eat. I remember asking her if she had ever been to West Point. She said she had not, but that her mother had gone on dates "up there" at one time. I told her I would be delighted to invite her up at some time, but she gave me an evasive answer. Nevertheless, we exchanged addresses and phone numbers.

Our relationship got off to a rocky start, but the worst was yet to come. Later, in the summer when I was training Yearling cadets at Camp Buckner, the nearby training site on the West Point reservation, I sent her a letter and invited her up for a weekend. She accepted. Then, lo and behold, at the last minute my mother sent me a telegram that she would arrive that same weekend, along with her brother, Bill, who lived nearby in the Pocono Mountains of Pennsylvania.

I tried to call Judy to explain the complicated situation, but apparently had miscopied her phone number. Since she was due to arrive the next day, I sent her a telegram with a rather curt message to the effect that "Mother will arrive unexpectedly, please let's postpone the weekend." I also asked her to call me so I could explain. The reason was logistics: there was only so much time on weekends and my mother and uncle would consume most of it. However, Judy did not get the message until the next day while she was at work at the FBI, along with her packed suitcase.

Of course, Judy was dumbfounded, wondering what she almost had gotten into. She went home in a huff. Thanks to her mother, we weathered that storm and reconnected. Judy's mother had dated at West Point and told Judy she at least should give it another try because it was a unique place. Fortunately for me, one of my classmates had an illegal car and also a girlfriend in Washington. From time to time, I would share the expense of a ride to Washington with him so that I could see Judy. When she finally did get to meet my mother, they hit it off right away.

Judy's family consisted of her father, William, who was an illustrator for the Red Cross, her mother, Lydia, an older sister, also Lydia, but we called her Skip, and a younger brother, William Jr. We began on-and-off dating and as First Class year wore on, we began to get serious about marriage.

Upon graduation, we were married in June of 1956 (Figure 8), and spent our honeymoon at Siesta Key, Florida, in a cottage my mother had arranged for us. Mother also arranged for the same cottage to be used by another classmate, George Loffert and his new bride, Gloria, for their honeymoon.

After graduation in June 1956, I was commissioned as a second lieutenant (2LT) of Armor in the Regular Army. Walt was commissioned as a second lieutenant in the USAF and Bill was commissioned as a 2LT of Armor in the Regular Army.

As for Uncle Bill's place in the Poconos, after Judy and I were married and I was teaching at West Point, we would often go there to spend weekends.

Fig. 8 Jim and Judy's marriage

CHAPTER 3

Initial Military Training

After a month's leave, Judy and I reported to Fort Knox, Kentucky, home of the U.S. Army Armor School, as students in the Armor Officers Basic Course. The course was designed to make a newly commissioned officer proficient in the skills necessary to be a successful small unit armor leader. This was the first of three tours I would serve at Fort Knox.

Since Judy had not finished her degree work at George Washington University (GWU), shortly after we arrived at Fort Knox, she returned to Washington to continue work on her degree in elementary education. I then moved into the BOQ (Bachelor Officer Quarters).

After several months at Fort Knox and completion of the course, Judy and I now reunited, moved to Fort Benning, Georgia, for training at the Army Ranger School. The two-month Ranger Course began at Fort Benning, then moved to the Georgia mountains, and finished with amphibious training at Fort Walton Beach, Florida.

In addition to the training rigors, our course fought a continuous battle with the elements. We arrived at Fort Benning late in the year after winter had set in. On one frigid occasion, after we had forded the Upatoi Creek, we were scheduled to climb to the top of a nearby 50-foot high cliff using ropes. However, the creek water that had collected on our clothes and on our hands had turned to ice on the ropes, making them unusable. In the end, we finally walked around the cliff to get to the top. On another occasion in the Georgia mountains, on a combat patrol exercise problem, we did not take along enough cold weather gear and we had to stuff dead leaves in our clothing to provide enough insulation to stay warm.

Ranger training consisted of a series of small unit actions. The class was divided up into "patrols" of 10–12 men, who would work together as a team to solve a particular tactical requirement or problem. Ranger School provided the best small unit leadership training I had ever received in the Army. It taught teamwork, resourcefulness, basic leadership skills and the requirement for decisiveness. By decisiveness, I mean when there is a requirement to do something tactically and there is no real good answer, be proactive and do something. Force the issue. Don't wait until all the pieces fall into place. However, I also have to say that sometimes choosing to do nothing is also an option, but it is the choice that is important. All in all, Ranger training was some of the very best training a junior officer could receive.

After Ranger School, we had qualified in airborne training (jump school). As a result of the Ranger training, we were all in tip-top physical shape, so we took the rigors of jump school in stride. Jump school was also conducted at Fort Benning. It was a six-week course that taught us how to jump from an airplane onto a drop zone. In addition to conditioning exercises for those who needed to get into better shape, we were trained in how to land without hurting ourselves, what to do if we landed in trees (I did twice), and how to load and unload cargo aircraft.

All of the jumps were "static line" jumps. A static line is a strap that that is hooked to a wire inside of the aircraft so that when one exits the aircraft, the strap opens the backpack parachute automatically when the jumper is a sufficient distance from the aircraft. Each jumper also wore a chest pack reserve parachute that could be opened manually by a ripcord in case the main parachute malfunctioned. In those days, we did not make free-fall jumps. To make a free-fall jump, you pulled your own ripcord after you left the aircraft. Free-fall jumping is now taught as part of Ranger School. I made the required eight jumps and thus called myself an "eight-jump commando." I have not jumped out of an aircraft since!

Initial Assignments

In the spring of 1957, Judy and I reported to F Company (later re-designated as G Troop), 2nd Squadron, 2nd Armored Cavalry Regiment (2ACR) at Fort Meade, Maryland. At that time, the 2ACR was an Operation Gyroscope unit. Operation Gyroscope rotated units in the United States with units in Europe as part of a NATO (North Atlantic Treaty Organization) plan, usually every three years. The 2ACR was scheduled to replace the 3ACR on the East-West German border in the spring of 1958.

In the spring of 1957, the 2ACR was at "cadre strength," which meant that the unit had most of its officers and NCOs, but very few soldiers. As a result, my initial duties revolved around training recruits who would flesh out our unit. Training underclassmen at West Point had well prepared me for this task.

In May 1957, our daughter, Cheryl Lyn, was born (Figure 1). Shortly thereafter, I was selected to lead the F Company advance party to Bamberg, Germany, to begin the rather arduous task of transferring vehicles and other property between the 2ACR and 3ACR. In October 1957 my growing family embarked on a Lockheed Constellation at nearby Baltimore International Airport for our flight to Nuremberg, Germany. Cheryl was in diapers and Judy was pregnant with our soon-to-be son, Scott. We made stops at Gander, Newfoundland, and Shannon, Ireland before landing at Nuremberg.

Fig. 1 Cheryl Lyn as a baby

At Nuremberg, we were met by our hosts from the 3ACR who bused us to Bamberg and helped settle us into military housing. We then began the work associated with rotating units.

The transfer of Army property and responsibility for policing the East-West German border went relatively smoothly. Our squadron headquarters was at Bamberg. The 1st Squadron was headquartered at Bayreuth, the 3rd Squadron at Amberg and the Regimental HQ at Nuremberg. In those days, the 2nd Squadron consisted of three reconnaissance (recon) troops, a tank company and a howitzer battery. An assignment to an ACR was a great early experience for a young officer and stood me in good stead later in my career when I was assigned to combined arms teams. An ACR was a true combined arms team: Armor, Infantry and Artillery.

One of our three recon troops, augmented by personnel from the tank company and howitzer battery, would move to our border station in Coburg, Germany, every four to six weeks. From Coburg we would establish observation posts (OPs) and run roving patrols along the border. In addition to policing the border, we trained to fulfill our wartime mission of screening and delaying an assault by Warsaw Pact forces.

Prior to the end of WWII in Europe, the allied powers (principally the U.S., U.K., France and Russia) divided Germany into occupation zones so that at the end of the war, there was shared responsibility for administering the rehabilitation of the country. West Germany was administered by the U.K., France and the U.S. Soviet Russia administered what became East Germany. The Western Allies instituted the Marshall Plan, named after Secretary of State George Marshall. This was a very successful plan designed to reinvigorate Western Europe politically and economically after the war. This arrangement soon broke down on the Soviet side, though, as the Soviets began to ransack their occupied zone in Germany for industrial equipment. The Soviets also began to install communist governments. They did this not only in their part of Germany, but also in the countries eastward toward the Soviet Union.

By the 1950s, the Cold War had started. On one side, the Western Allies formed NATO. On the other side, the Soviets formed the Warsaw Pact, which included all of those countries in Eastern Europe in which they had installed communist governments. At one point, the U.S. had garrisoned over 300,000 soldiers, sailors and airmen in NATO countries, mainly in Germany, the Mediterranean and the U.K. In addition, the United States began REFORGER (REnFORcement of units in GERmany) exercises designed to rapidly reinforce NATO from the United States in the event of an imminent Soviet threat.

Troop Command

After a year or so as platoon leader and troop executive officer (2nd in command), I was promoted to commanding officer (CO) of G Troop. F

Company had been re-designated as G Troop in late 1958. By this time, I was a first lieutenant (1LT). I assumed command of G Troop in early 1959, after our squadron CO, Lieutenant Colonel (LTC) Woodson was replaced by LTC John R. Whittick, one of the most professional officers with whom I would ever serve. After he got his feet on the ground, LTC Whittick made some needed personnel changes.

As a result of one of these changes, I replaced Captain Rohry MacNeill (a micromanager) as commander of G Troop. LTC Whittick considered Captain MacNeill better suited to be a staff officer. The first thing I did was go to work reorganizing G Troop. The troop had excellent officers and NCOs (many were WWII veterans), but they weren't allowed to perform up to their abilities. I decentralized both authority and responsibility to the appropriate level, which caused a rapid improvement in the professionalism of the unit. This was to be my first experience in turning around a group that was underperforming. In April 1958, our son, Scott (Figure 2), was born in the Nuremberg Hospital.

LTC Whittick had promised me at least a year as a troop commander, a much sought-after position, and he was true to his word. After a little more than a year as a troop CO, LTC Whittick made me squadron adjutant (S-1), a position which required me to work very closely with him. I learned much from him about attention to detail, military justice, and the importance of smooth, coordinated staff work. LTC Whittick was a prior horse cavalryman who, after a period of weak leadership, quickly steered

the entire 2nd Squadron in the right direction. He previously had a close relationship with our regimental commander, Colonel Bud Schlanser, who was probably instrumental in getting LTC Whittick assigned to the 2nd Squadron.

Externally, we improved the efficiency of our border operations by more closely coordinating with the other squadrons and by conducting more maneuver exercises. Internally, as S-1, I was responsible for

Fig. 2 Jim with baby Scott

every staff action that crossed the boss's desk. He gave me, a mere 1LT who was dealing with majors and captains, full authority to kick back an incomplete staff action, a military justice case or other personnel matter. I was also responsible for the operation and location of our command post (CP) while on maneuvers in the field.

Fig. 3 Jim with LTC Whittick

LTC Whittick also recognized the importance of families. Since one of our three recon troops was always away at our border camp at Coburg, families were often separated. He had the staff organize bowling leagues, birthday celebrations and children's athletic teams. In the picture above (Figure 3), LTC Whittick is presenting me a bowling trophy. We also had an officers' softball team that would compete against other units stationed at Bamberg. In short, he rebuilt 2nd Squadron both professionally and socially. As a result, I learned the value of involved, no-nonsense leadership. Years later, I would apply some of LTC Whittick's leadership techniques when I was placed in command of a similar squadron that had previously experienced weak leadership.

In April 1961, Judy, family and I rotated back to Fort Knox, Kentucky for further training in the Armor Officer Advanced Course, a nine-month long course designed to train junior officers as troop commanders and junior staff officers. Since I had already been a troop commander and a junior staff officer, the course served to put polish on jobs I had already experienced. I was promoted to captain (CPT) while at Fort Knox.

Return to West Point

It was at Fort Knox that I was contacted by the Department of Mechanics at West Point regarding my returning as a professor in the Department of Mechanics. Judy and I discussed the opportunity and decided to accept it. The Department of Mechanics gave me three choices for graduate school: MIT, the University of Michigan or the

University of Arizona. Neither Judy nor I had lived in the southwestern U.S. before, so we chose the University of Arizona (U of A), located at Tucson. Judy took advantage of our stay in Tucson to continue work on her degree in elementary education. She had discontinued her degree work at George Washington University (GWU) when we were assigned to Europe. When she learned we would be attending the U of A, she worked out a program with George Washington to continue and complete her coursework at the University of Arizona.

I graduated from the U of A in June 1964 with a master's degree in aerospace engineering. I was asked by the Department of Mechanics at U of A to do my master's thesis on the calibration of the school's new variable throat supersonic wind tunnel, which I did. It was hands-on work and I thoroughly enjoyed doing it. One of my instrumentation professors had been a member of Draper Laboratories at MIT during WWII and had helped develop torpedoes during the war. My thesis for him was built around designing a weather station on the planet Jupiter.

At the U of A, I also learned tolerance and a different view of racism. One of my Black engineering classmates (Cliff Worthy) was a West Point graduate, several years ahead of me, who had been my mentor on the tennis and squash teams at West Point. Segregation was still rampant at that time, so Cliff asked Judy and me to help him find a place to live. It turned out that being Black was not a problem for local landlords; being Hispanic was. We found him a nice place with no problem. At this time, U of A was trying to become the MIT of the Southwest, so the courses were difficult. We formed study groups with other military students so that we could tutor each other. As a result, all of us graduated with master's degrees.

After graduation, my family and I drove directly to West Point for new instructor training. Our quarters were not quite ready for occupancy, so Judy and the children stayed in Washington, D.C. with her parents while she completed her coursework at George Washington University. Two other geographic bachelors and I stayed in the living quarters of a Department of Mechanics instructor, who was away for the summer studying for his doctorate. When our quarters were ready, Judy and the kids drove up and we moved into our new on base home.

Quarters selection day at West Point was one of the best shows in town. It takes place in mid-summer, and back then it was held in a large auditorium. Even people who already had quarters came to watch the show. Date of rank and even class standing meant everything. The available quarters were posted on 3-by-5 cards on a large portable blackboard. Of course, participants had a paper copy in their hands of what was available. The most senior person got first choice and that card was pulled from the blackboard. As the number of available quarters diminished and selection came down to class standing, some of those seeking a particular unit that had already been taken often became very emotional. It was not unusual for a wife, who did not get the quarters she wanted, to yell at her husband with words such as, "Why didn't you study harder?"

Back at West Point, I thoroughly enjoyed being an instructor at my alma mater. Later during this tour, I was advanced to an assistant professor in the Department of Mechanics. I taught thermodynamics and fluid mechanics, mostly to Cows (juniors), but also to some Yearlings (sophomores) as well.

It was standard procedure to grade the cadets every day. A classroom period would start with an opportunity for students to ask questions about the previous session's homework. This was where the teaching/instruction was done. However, the onus was still on the cadets to come to class at least ready and able to ask pertinent questions. The sources available while doing homework were pretty extensive, so the students had suitable materials for reference. During the evening's study hours, cadets would prepare for at least four classes the next day. In the afternoons we provided extra instruction for those who needed it. When the questions were cleared up, cadets would each go to chalkboards to solve problems related to the homework.

At the end of the period, homework for the next lesson was assigned and the board work graded (after the cadets had left the classroom). About every six weeks, the classroom sections were shuffled; cadets with the highest grades (Hives) going to the upper sections, which required less classroom instruction. Those with lower grades (Goats) would end up in the lower sections. This system allowed instructors to tailor their instruction to the abilities of the students. I enjoyed working with the Goats, as it was most gratifying to see a light of understanding suddenly dawn in a cadet's eyes. Most of the other departments at West Point used the same system.

West Point was also a good family post. Cheryl and Scott were able to walk to the nearby elementary school. Judy became involved in Little Theater as well as activities with the Officers' Wives Club. I coached Little League Baseball and we both joined a bowling league. I coached my son, Scott's, Little League Baseball team of 6- to 8-year-olds. We had "daddy pitchers," whose job was to hit the bat. Regretfully, as so often happens with teams of boys/girls that age, we had two things working against us: a railroad track and parents. Our Little League field was alongside a railroad track. If a ball was in the air when a train came by, all action ceased as the kids watched the train. Also, parents would actively give their sons advice from the stands regarding what they should do on the field. Judy was no exception. She became so vocal telling Scott what to do that it became disruptive. In desperation, I made her scorekeeper. This tended to keep her quiet.

The only downside to duty at West Point was that it took me out of Army mainstream duties for five years (two years of grad school, plus three years at the academy). During this time, a number of my classmates who stayed in mainstream assignments were selected for "below the zone" (accelerated) promotions. I would later catch up, but at the time, it was frustrating. However, I was promoted to major (MAJ) while at West Point. The war in Vietnam had started by this time (1965), and some of my classmates who had been in combat were promoted to major before me.

Command and General Staff College

During my last year at West Point (1966–1967), I was selected to attend the Army Command and General Staff College (CGSC) at Fort Leavenworth, Kansas. At about the same time, I was also told by the Armor Officers Assignment Branch that I could expect to go to Vietnam after completion of CGSC. The latter was great news for me. Most of my classmates were serving in Vietnam or had already served there. By this time, action was getting hot in Southeast Asia and I didn't want to miss it.

As a combat arms officer, serving in combat was the goal most of us sought. Many of us already had a great deal of schooling in *how* to fight, but up until this time, few had actually been in combat. I was eager to find out if all of my training had adequately prepared me for actual wartime missions. The Army schooling system not only well-prepared us for our combat tasks, but also it gave us a feeling of accomplishment. We found out that our tactical doctrine was solid, and as a result, we were very good at what we were doing.

A large part of the curriculum at CGSC was devoted to staff work in large organizations. As it turned out, it was perfect preparation for the assignment I would receive in Vietnam, where I would eventually become the operations officer (S-3) of the 11th ACR (armored cavalry regiment), the Blackhorse Regiment. I did not know at the time, but the regimental commander, Colonel George Patton, son of the famous WWII General Patton, had asked that I be assigned to that regiment.

Assignment to the CGSC was also a good family posting. The kids had good schools and Judy continued to be involved in Little Theater. We also became members of a mixed doubles bowling league and won the league championship.

After graduation from CGSC in June, Read Hanmer (a fellow instructor in the Department of Mechanics who attended CGSC at the same time as me, and who was also headed for Vietnam) and I relocated our families to Hampton, Virginia. As it turned out, Judy and Lois Hanmer had grown up together in Washington, D.C. By this time, both our children and the Hanmer children had formed very close friendships, which endure to this day. After getting the family settled in a rental townhouse in Hampton, I headed west to Travis AFB, California, to catch a military charter flight, stopping in Sonoma to visit our West Point duplex neighbor friends Bob and Marilyn Elton.

CHAPTER 4

Combat Duty With the 11th ACR in Vietnam

Following the military charter flight from Travis, my tour in Vietnam got off to an unexpected start. In July, I arrived at Bien Hoa Air Base (Figure 1), near Long Binh, north of Saigon, Vietnam. I was met by a friend from 2ACR days, Major Al Pankowski, who informed me that my assignment had changed. He said, laughing, that I would be his "turtle," or replacement. I was no longer headed to the 11th ACR, but to the Adjutant General's (AG) section of HQ USARV (U.S. Army Vietnam) where I would assign combat arms majors, as he had done. I vigorously protested, to no avail.

I worked in the AG section for a couple of months assigning majors. It was mostly desk work, but I learned a lot about how the Army personnel system worked. I also learned that the CG (commanding general), USARV, LTG Mildren, was serious about keeping the staffing of the HQ at a reasonable level. He felt that if not closely watched, HQ staffs tended to grow on their own. Periodically, when staffing reached a certain level, he would order a reduction. I took advantage of one of those periodic reductions to assign myself to a combat unit. After discussion with my boss, LTC Bartlett, we agreed that my job at HQ USARV could be combined with that of the officer who assigned combat arms LTCs (lieutenant colonels). I was thus able to assign myself to the 11th ACR, with whom I had previously coordinated.

My service with the 11th ACR marked a turning point in my military career. I found that all of my previous training had well-prepared me for combat. I put that training to good use almost immediately.

As previously mentioned, the regiment was commanded by Colonel George S. Patton III, son of the famous WWII General Patton. He had what I would later call "battle sense," the instinct to do the right thing at the right time in combat. Not all combat leaders have that instinct, a fact I quickly learned while serving with Patton, and compared as well to other less capable commanders with whom we interacted.

Fig. 1 Vietnam map

He would have a profound impact on my future military career. He, in effect became my mentor. Colonel Patton was cut out of the same cloth as his father.

My relationship with George Patton began while I was a cadet at West Point. At that time, he was a company tactical officer of a cadet company. As a cadet at the time, I did not have a close relationship with him. He had the reputation among cadets, though, of being brusque, but tough, fair and well-respected. Later, while I was with the 2ACR commanding G Troop on the border of East-West Germany, he visited us several times while he was an aide to LTG Farrell, our corps commander. On each visit he would discuss the various aspects of commanding a reconnaissance unit. These were open discussions with both officers and enlisted soldiers of things that he saw which were both good and bad. He thoroughly enjoyed talking to enlisted soldiers. I learned quite a bit about leadership from him. Apparently, he liked what he saw in G Troop, because we were always one of his stops during border tours.

In Vietnam, as soon as my transfer to the 11th ACR was official, I was picked up by a courier driver at HQ USARV and driven to the 11th ACR's temporary HQ on the airbase at Bien Hoa. I was welcomed by Colonel Patton (Figure 2) and several other officers with whom I had previously served. However, since the Bien Hoa HQ was a temporary HQ, I was flown by a Huey helicopter to our permanent Base Camp at Xuan Loc. After being in-processed at the Base Camp, I was initially assigned as an assistant operations officer in the operations section (S-3) working under a classmate, LTC Bill Haponski.

Fig. 2 Colonel George Patton

To orient me on the operations of the regiment, I spent the first week or so flying around our area of operations (AO) with our plans officer, Captain Dick Allen, a Chemical Corps officer, who had an aptitude for combat operations. Each morning we would take off in a light observation helicopter (LOH) to visit each unit in the regiment. Dick would discuss current operations with each unit's commander or S-3 staffs. He would later use this information at the regimental evening briefing, bringing Colonel Patton and the staff further insights into what was going on in the regiment, as well as outlining the next day's activities.

The travels with Dick Allen gave me an invaluable, keen insight into the activities of the regiment. We would usually get back to the HQ about noon, after which I would spend the rest of the day getting acquainted with the operations of the tactical operations center (TOC), the hub of regimental activities. I also had time to get to know the members of the regimental staff.

The regimental executive officer (XO) was LTC Larry Wright, who commanded the Base Camp at Xuan Loc and whom I would run into several times throughout the remainder of my career.

Regimental Staff

Regimental S-1: Dale Hruby, a West Point grad.

Regimental S-2: Andy O'Meara, another West Point grad with whom I would serve in the future.

Regimental S-3: Bill Haponski, a classmate, who would eventually command a reconnaissance squadron in the 1st Infantry Division (1st ID).

Regimental S-4: Glenn Finkbiner, an old friend with whom I would also serve several times in the future.

Air Cavalry Troop Commander: John "Doc" Bahnsen, another classmate with whom I would also serve in the future.

TOC Officer-in-Charge (OIC): Jerry Rutherford, an assistant S-3 who ran the TOC, and who would later retire as a LTG corps commander.

All of these officers were exceptionally well-qualified, fine soldiers. Colonel Patton had an eye for talent and it showed in the makeup of his key staff.

After several weeks as an assistant S-3, Bill Haponski left the regiment for his command tour with the 1st Infantry Division (ID) and I became the S-3 with Jerry Rutherford as my assistant.

When I first arrived in the regiment, our AO was north of Bien Hoa in what were called War Zones C and D. We were what I called the Fire Brigade for II Field Force, a corps-sized HQ responsible for an area north of Saigon, between the Saigon River and the Cambodian border.

Initially, our primary enemy was a Viet Cong (VC) unit known as the Dong Ngai Regiment, which recruited from villages in our AO. It had a very able commander and tough soldiers. Since most of its members were recruited from local villages, they knew the terrain extremely well. But this was also a disadvantage for them. Often between operations, their members would venture back to their home villages to spend some time with their families. Once we became aware of this, we would set up ambushes, catching them going or coming. This would usually precipitate a larger action that would allow us to use our pile-on tactics and superior firepower.

During roughly the second half of my tour, we fought mainly North Vietnamese Army (NVA) units who had infiltrated down the Ho Chi Minh Trail in Laos and Cambodia and then into South Vietnam. Our tactics remained the same (See map, Figure 1). We would intercept the enemy, then bring our superior firepower and mobility to bear. We would pick them up as they crossed the Cambodian border, fight them for a while and then turn the remnants over to an ARVN (Army of the Republic of South Vietnam) unit to finish them off. ARVN units by this time had developed into pretty good fighting organizations. Early on in the war, our leadership put forth a special effort to train all of the South Vietnamese military. These efforts were beginning to pay off during my tour in 1968–69. They became progressively better during subsequent years, and by the early 1970s, were more than able to hold their own. They were so effective by this time that the VC were unable to recruit. Of course, the North Vietnamese were aware of this, which precipitated their eventual wholesale invasion of the South.

My Views Regarding U.S. Involvement in Vietnam

I continue to be embarrassed by our precipitant departure and lack of support for the Republic of South Vietnam (RVN). Due largely to misguided U.S. political leadership, we snatched defeat from the jaws of victory. After a number of fits and starts by the Johnson Administration, we had helped the RVN defeat the insurgency by entering the war. We had helped them rebuild their armed forces, but when the NVA invaded the South, we withdrew all types of support at the worst possible time. In effect, we allowed the NVA to defeat the RVN. However, our sacrifices of men and material were not totally in vain. As was the case with a less than total victory in the Korean War, we stopped the spread of communism in Southeast Asia.

With several exceptions, I will not discuss specific combat actions in which I was involved. Those are well-covered in another book written by my classmate Doc Bahnsen with Wess Roberts, titled *American Warrior*.

It is extremely well-documented, and I had the opportunity to contribute quite a bit to the research. It covers in detail many of the combat actions in which I was personally involved. Instead, I will dwell on my relationship with Colonel Patton and how we went about performing our various missions.

Here are the three exceptions:

While with Patton and a number of our subordinate commanders and staff, I was standing on some high ground, observing one of our armored units attacking VC. The VC were dug in along a treeline across a wide open

Fig. 3 Award of Purple Heart by MG Davidson

area several hundred yards wide. Suddenly, there was an explosion in the middle of our group of about six to eight. It was probably caused by a VC mortar round. Most likely some alert VC mortar crew had spotted us as a good target. I was the only one hit. The others were completely unscathed. I received a fragment wound in my left forearm, which began to bleed profusely. Patton, himself, started first aid to stop the bleeding, then loaded me into his own helicopter and flew me to the 93rd Evacuation Hospital at Bien Hoa. (More on the 93rd Evacuation Hospital later.) I stayed in the hospital overnight while my wound was cleaned up and treated. I was released the next day and had to wear that arm in a sling for about a week. I was subsequently awarded the Purple Heart (Figure 3) at an evening 11th ACR staff briefing by Major General Mike Davidson, who was then visiting us. I had gotten to know General Davidson at West Point when he was a tactical officer and I was a cadet.

The second exception is with regard to being awarded the Silver Star, which I didn't think I deserved. During my first tour in the Pentagon, I was contacted by recently retired Colonel Jimmy Leach, the colonel who succeeded Patton in command of the 11th ACR. He told me that he was

remiss in not recommending me for a Silver
Star for my performance during a certain
combat action while under his command.
The event occurred near the Cambodian
border, just prior to the end of my tour with
the 11th ACR (Figure 4). It was during one
of those times when he was overseeing one
action, and I, in another helicopter, was overseeing another. I don't know how he found
out about it; maybe some of those involved
told him after I had departed. To me, it was
sort of routine, in that I had been in more
dangerous actions while with Patton. See
award of Silver Star by MG (Major General) Bolton in Figure 5.

Fig. 4 Jim with COL
Leach in Vietnam

I was in an OH-58 light observation heli-
copter (LOH), flown by LT Bert Dacey, who was later killed in action
(KIA). We were assisting one of our units, a recon troop commanded by
a captain, in contact with a good-sized NVA force in pretty thick jungle.
As I recall, the NVA were defending a base camp and supply storage area.
The unit on the ground was "jungle busting" with their larger vehicles,
protected by infantry units in their lighter vehicles. I was providing aerial
observation and coordinating support (artillery and air). Since the unit
commander was on the ground with his unit and had very little forward
visibility, it was up to me to keep him headed in the right direction in
such thick jungle.

At one point, Dacey and I noted that one platoon had become separated from the remainder of the troop and had exposed its flank to a
large enemy force in a bunker complex. I tried unsuccessfully to contact
the troop commander by radio. We then flew at low level over the enemy
position so that our door gunner could engage the NVA with machine-
gun fire. After several firing passes and still unable to contact the unit
on the ground, we landed in a small, nearby clearing. I found the platoon leader and explained the situation to him. Two of his vehicles had
been damaged by NVA antitank fire. We then reorganized and assaulted
the enemy position, clearing it of NVA. After the wounded had been

evacuated, Dacey and I took off again to direct the platoon as it rejoined the rest of the troop.

It was then obvious that the NVA were there with a much larger force than we first expected. "Pile-on tactics" were then applied. The squadron commander reinforced his recon troop in contact with additional forces. I called in more artillery fire and tactical air support (TACAIR). As a result, we overran an important NVA position and destroyed quite a large force and tons of supplies.

A third exception is with regard to a helicopter door gunner who was awarded the Congressional Medal of Honor.

So that he could get out and participate in some action, I was spelling Jerry Rutherford (Figure 6), who was normally in the TOC. During a rou-

Fig. 5 Award of Silver Star by MG Bolton with Judy

Fig. 6 Jim with Jerry Rutherford

tine contact with the enemy, I heard Doc Bahnsen, our Air Cav troop commander, broadcast on the radio: "I'm on fire and going in." I knew that Jerry was involved in that action, so I asked him what was going on. He said that he was following Doc's helicopter in his orbit over the contact, and it looked like a white phosphorous (WP) grenade had gone off in the aircraft. That is exactly what happened.

Unknown to most of us, Doc was taking his girlfriend and future wife, Fif, a State Department contract employee stationed in Saigon, on an unauthorized helicopter ride that day, when the mission was called in. Unable to land and safely offload Fif, he proceeded to the mission area, ready to do battle. When directed to do so, it was a common procedure for the door gunners to mark targets with WP grenades. A door gunner named Yano had pulled the pin on a WP grenade prior to throwing it out of the aircraft. When the aircraft banked the other way, Yano, gripping the handle so it wouldn't go off, tried to hand the grenade to the other door gunner on the other side of the aircraft, but dropped it, releasing the handle. It exploded in the helicopter, burning everyone on board, including Doc and Fif.

The WP also set fire to the ammunition and the other cases of grenades stacked in the aircraft. Courageously, Yano began kicking and throwing the burning ordnance out of the aircraft. While doing so, he was seriously burned over most of his body, particularly his hands, which were burned to the bone. However, he kept going until the aircraft was clear of all burning material. For his heroic actions that day, Yano, who later died from his injuries, was posthumously awarded the Congressional Medal of Honor.

Doc did not crash the helicopter, but managed to fly it to the 93rd Evacuation Hospital in Bien Hoa, not far from our HQ. When he got there, and after his and Fif's wounds were treated, the hospital put him in the men's ward and Fif in the female ward. Doc, a major at the time, demanded that he and Fif be put into the same ward. Of course, the hospital personnel refused. Doc escalated the issue to the hospital commander, a colonel. That is when I got involved.

Fortunately for Doc, George Patton was in Hawaii on R & R (rest and relaxation) at the time. The hospital commander's office called the nearby 11th ACR saying that the commander immediately wanted to talk to Colonel Patton about one of his majors. Our regimental executive officer, LTC Merritt Ireland, was nowhere to be found. So, that left two of us majors to answer the call. The caller said that Major Doc Bahnsen was raising hell in the hospital, invoking the name of Colonel Patton, and that the hospital commander wanted someone from the 11th ACR to report to his office right away. My friend Glenn Finkbiner and I matched out and I lost.

I drove over to the hospital in a jeep and reported to the hospital commander. He was livid. He didn't tell me to stand at ease or sit down. He asked if I knew the history of the Patton family and the 93rd Evac. Regretfully, I did not. He told me that this was the same hospital in which Colonel Patton's father had slapped a soldier in Sicily during WWII, and he didn't want to go through another Patton episode.

I told him I would take care of the problem, saluted and left to visit Doc, Fif and Yano in the same hospital. Doc and Fif had rather serious WP burns. Yano was very badly injured and under heavy sedation. His hands were wrapped in gauze, his face was blackened, and he could hardly speak. I told him he could be very proud of what he had done. He acknowledged that.

Yano died shortly thereafter and was buried in the Punch Bowl Cemetery in Hawaii.

When Patton returned from R & R and was briefed on the event, he immediately went to the hospital, chewed out Doc royally and had Fif transferred to a Saigon hospital. This was the type of leader and commander Colonel Patton was. He had every right to relieve Doc, send him back to the states and end his career. Instead, he recognized Doc's warfighting ability and gave him another chance to prove himself and win back his respect. This, Doc did.

Patton's Leadership Approach

Colonel Patton's leadership approach was much like his dad's: Lead from the front. In the regiment we also adopted the slogan, "Find the Bastards and Pile On." We aggressively went after the enemy.

We used our air cavalry troop in a true reconnaissance role as called for by Army doctrine. They were often the first to find the enemy, attack them, and hold them in place until reinforcements arrived. In addition, they had Cobra gunships and an Aero Rifle Platoon. This gave the troop commander tremendous flexibility and combat power.

Patton usually spent his day in a helicopter, visiting units and their commanders. Unless there were several combat actions (contacts) going on, I was usually with him. In addition to Patton and me, our helicopter crew consisted of our pilot, Warrant Officer (WO) Charlie Watkins, a copilot, two door gunners, and Command Sergeant Major (CSM) Mulcahy, later CSM Squires after Mulcahy was wounded and medically evacuated.

If we had a real big operation in progress, we would also carry an artillery coordinator with us. If there were multiple actions ongoing, I would oversee one while Patton was assisting the other. Our job was to assist the commander on the ground by making his job easier, both by anticipating needs and also integrating his actions with those of others. We would also be in radio contact with an Air Force forward air controller (FAC). Thus, we were in a position to give the commander on the ground whatever support he needed. If he needed an airstrike, we could arrange that with the FAC. If reinforcements were required, we would have them standing by ready to roll or fly. Since we had a better view of a combat action than those on the ground in dense jungle, we could direct the overall movement of units.

For instance, on one occasion, we had two friendly units shooting at each other across a small clearing. When our air cavalry troop CO, Doc Bahnsen, became aware of this, he radioed both unit commanders, "When I land to your front, cease fire." Fortunately for Doc, they did and fratricide was avoided.

My specific job was to manage combat support (artillery, air, gunships, etc.). I did this using the command radios in the helicopter. The CSM's job was to monitor the radios and call our attention to radio traffic that he felt was important and that we had not heard. We habitually monitored three communication nets: the regimental command net, the command net of the troops in contact, and the fire request net. Patton seldom interfered with the actions of a commander on the ground unless things got really complicated. Back in the TOC, Jerry Rutherford would be monitoring the radios and anticipating needs. Often, a commander would call for an airstrike or a gunship and Jerry would answer that they were already on the way.

From time to time, we would work with the 1st Infantry Division, the 1st Cavalry Division and various Army of Vietnam (ARVN) units. We usually would have an ARVN Ranger Battalion attached to us. They were good fighters and provided excellent intelligence, and we developed a mutual respect for each other.

One of the ARVN Ranger Battalions attached to the 11th ACR was commanded by a middle-aged Vietnamese captain, who had been fighting for his country's freedom for most of his adult life. One day when we entered his base camp mess hall, we saw a sign (Figure 7) displayed in the national colors of the Republic of Vietnam: red, green and gold. The commander was thanking us because there were two American advisors helping his battalion fight for the freedom of his country. The moral I took away from the sign is that freedom is not free. It is always worth fighting for. I firmly believe that.

The philosophy portrayed by that sign continues to guide my view of where our country fits into the international order. The United States is a superpower. As columnist Joe Jophe once stated in a *Wall Street Journal* article, "A superpower has responsibilities." He further stated that "A superpower cannot go on vacation for even a little while." Our nation is a tremendous force for good on this planet. When we are actively involved, great things happen. When we don't get involved in key events, a leadership vacuum is created and tyrants quickly enter.

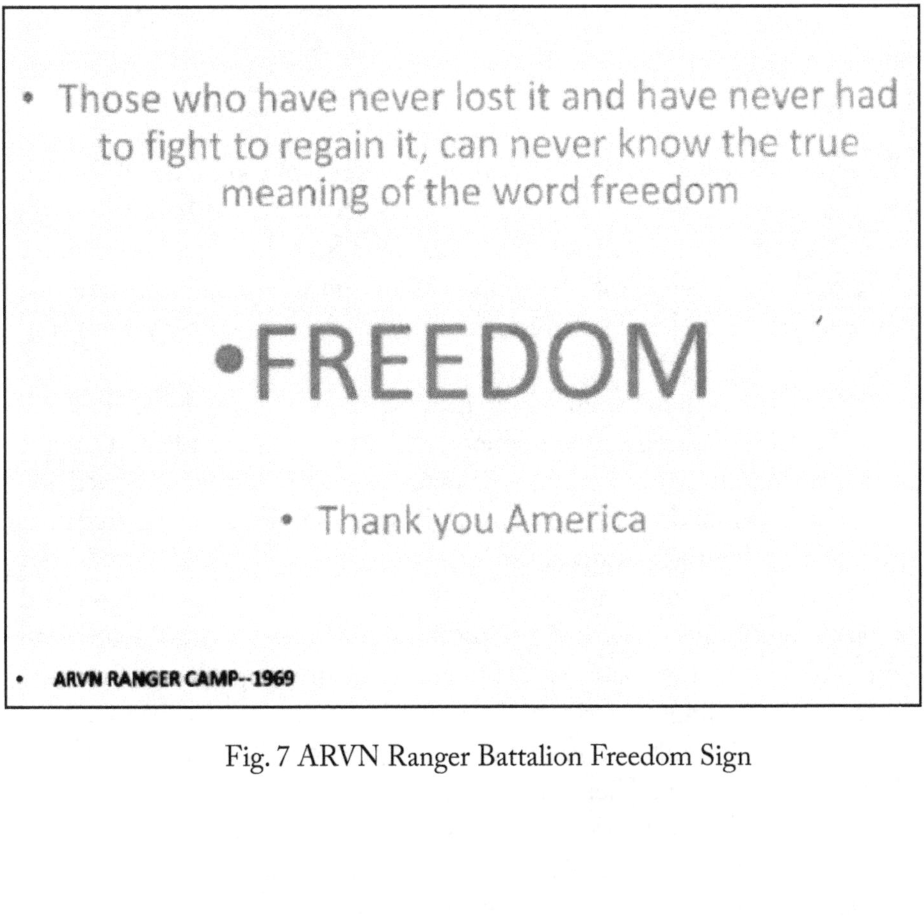

- Those who have never lost it and have never had to fight to regain it, can never know the true meaning of the word freedom

•FREEDOM

- Thank you America

• ARVN RANGER CAMP--1969

Fig. 7 ARVN Ranger Battalion Freedom Sign

CHAPTER 5

First Pentagon Tour

Early in July 1969, toward the end of my Vietnam tour, I was informed by the Armor Officer Assignment Branch that I would be assigned to the Pentagon in the Army Deputy Chief of Staff for Operations office (DCSOPS). When I told Judy about this, she was thrilled in that she once again would be close to her family, and she immediately went into house-hunting mode.

After a long flight from Vietnam, I called Judy from McCord AFB, near Seattle, Washington, to tell her that I was now stateside and to give her information on my flight to Washington, D.C. She informed me that she had found a nice house in Arlington, Virginia, not far from her friend Lois Hanmer's house. She also informed me that we would not go straight home after my arrival at National Airport, but that we had to stop by the title company to close on the house. After 36 hours with little to no sleep, I probably would have signed anything. When we finally reached our Arlington residence, I found it festooned with banners and signs welcoming me home. In those days that wasn't a typical welcome home ceremony for a Vietnam veteran.

In DCSOPS in the Pentagon, I was assigned to a current operations team called the Southeast Asia Team, made up of three officers plus two clerks. Our job was to stay on top of all Army operations in Southeast Asia and publish a summary each Monday morning. The team would brief the Secretary of the Army (Stanley Resor) daily, and brief the Army Chief of Staff (General William C. Westmoreland) each Monday before he went to the Joint Chiefs of Staff (JCS) meeting in the JCS conference room (The Tank, see Figure 1). It was

Fig.1 Jim as a Pentagon briefer

an interesting job and I learned much about the inner workings of the Department of Defense. My wife called the tour an accompanied "hardship tour." It was necessary to get to work early each day for our daily briefs. Since we had to work all weekend to prepare our Monday summary, our day off was Friday, which usually didn't coincide with family activities. Since we lived in Arlington, about 45 minutes from the Pentagon, commuting also took up a large portion of the day. Fortunately, Judy had many friends and family in the area, and Cheryl and Scott had good schools.

During my second year in the Pentagon, I was promoted to lieutenant colonel (O-5), and at the end of the year, Armor Branch notified me that I would soon be assigned to the First Armored Division (1st AD) in Germany. MG George Patton and I had formed a very close relationship in Vietnam, a sort of mentorship. I later learned that he had been instrumental in persuading Armor Branch to give me an opportunity to command the 1st Armored Division's Cavalry Squadron, a unit that was badly in need of better leadership.

It was a prestigious assignment. Patton would later be instrumental in providing me another turn-a-round assignment. This was already my third turn-a-round assignment. There would be others in my life, both in and out of the military. But those are different stories. Since our Pentagon tour had been so stressful, we decided that we would try to avoid another assignment in the Washington area and sold our home, which we later found out to be a big mistake.

Second Tour in Germany

We again headed to Germany in the spring of 1971. On arrival I was given a temporary assignment in Illesheim, Bavaria, Germany, where I was to be the brigade executive officer (XO) of the 2nd Brigade of the 1st Armored Division. This unit was commanded by Colonel John Byers, a soldier's soldier. Prior to my arrival, the brigade had been chosen to organize and lead the annual Division Tank Gunnery Program at Grafenwoehr, a large combined arms training area located in northern Bavaria.

Colonel Byers assigned me to oversee the gunnery program so that he could direct his efforts to leading the remainder of the large brigade, which consisted of two tank battalions, two infantry battalions and a divisional cavalry squadron. After getting the family settled in temporary quarters, I moved with a small staff (mostly our brigade S-3 Section) to Grafenwoehr, where I remained for the rest of the summer.

For an armored division, tank gunnery is a very important part of the training regimen. Commanders' careers can rise and fall based on how well the tank gunners shoot, so much emphasis was placed on training tankers. The final exam for a tank crew at Grafenwoehr included a successful negotiation of Range 80, a range with multiple pop-ups, stationary and moving targets, some of which are engaged while the tank is on the move.

It was a stressful course and tough to successfully negotiate. The targets were randomly activated by the range staff, not by the unit being tested. Usually, the "run" of a tank crew on the range was observed by the chain of command (battalion commander, brigade commander, sometimes even the division and corps commanders) from a control tower that overlooked the entire range. On one occasion, our Division CG, Major General (MG) James Galloway, turned to speak to a battalion commander whose unit was not shooting very well and asked him, "John, this is awful. Is there any reason that I should not relieve you of command right now?" Fortunately, he was given a second chance.

Squadron Command

In the early fall of 1971, I assumed command of the divisional cavalry squadron, re-designated a couple of times during my tour, but which I will call 1-1 Cavalry (1st Squadron, 1st Cavalry: the Blackhawks). The squadron was located at Schwabach, Germany, about an hour's drive from Illesheim. My family stayed in Illesheim while I moved to Schwabach, as my predecessor had not yet vacated his quarters at O'Brien Barracks, Schwabach.

I lived in the bachelor officer quarters (BOQ), above the officer's club for over a month. After G Troop, 2nd ACR and the S-3 Section of the 11th ACR, this would be my third opportunity to rebuild an organization that was not performing well. The 1-1 Cavalry was a large, dispersed unit. The HQ troop, plus A, B and C troops were at Schwabach, while there was an Air Cavalry troop at Katterbach, near the soon to be new Division HQ at Ansbach, about 30 miles away.

Our children, Cheryl and Scott, were bused to a high school in Nuremburg. This was the nearest military high school, about a 45-minute bus ride away. Scott (Figure 2) was not involved in any high school activities. Cheryl, however, became involved with the management of various high school athletic teams. She would sometimes stay overnight with Susan Graham, the daughter of our good friends Chuck and Alice Graham. Chuck commanded the 2ACR, headquartered in Nuremburg. From time to time, the 1-1 Cav would perform border duty for the 2ACR when the regiment was at a training area. We would later serve again with the Grahams at Fort Hood, Texas.

Fig. 2 Scott in high school

The early 1970s were a tough time to be a soldier in U.S. Army Europe (USAREUR). The war in Vietnam was still going strong and that theater rightly received priority of personnel, equipment, spare parts and other resources. In addition, in Europe there was a rampant drug problem among soldiers. Drugs were everywhere, supplied by a number of very sophisticated organizations, most of whom originated in the BENE-LUX countries (Belgium, Netherlands and Luxemburg). In addition, many of the distribution systems were organized by our own soldiers.

The drug problems were further aggravated by a shortage of experienced NCOs and officers. In some cases, a platoon, normally commanded by a lieutenant would be commanded by an NCO. A fully staffed chain of command was rare.

When I arrived at the unit, the chain of command was simply not functioning. In addition to the drug problems, morale was near rock bottom. My predecessor, a well-decorated Vietnam veteran, had kept the unit out of garrison and in the field as much as possible, in order to offset the drug problem. As a result, soldiers were away from their families more than was necessary and the vehicles had been run into the ground. I was aware of most of these problems before I arrived, but the overall magnitude surprised me. I had been warned by Colonel Byers that I would have my work cut out for me when I assumed command. He could not have been more accurate.

There was a bit of good news. The squadron Command Sergeant Major Raymond Garofalo was a thoroughly professional soldier. Shortly after I arrived, he and I had a chat about the unit. He was very frank about the status and he was right on target. In addition, Colonel Byers was able to get a new executive officer, Major Ski Manosky (Figure 3), assigned to the unit. Manosky was also a thoroughly professional soldier who had boundless energy and who worked well with soldiers. The three of us went to work.

I was aware that the unit was due to be comprehensively inspected by the 1st Armored Division inspector general (IG) about six weeks after I arrived. More than likely the inspection was scheduled in conjunction with my assuming command, even though I didn't know that. I figured that the inspection itself would give me a good baseline for starting to put the unit back on its feet, in addition to what I would learn myself in the weeks before the inspection. Lo and behold, the situation got worse.

Shortly after I arrived, Manosky and I were in the motor pool inspecting the "gunbooks" of the M-551 Sheridan light tanks. Gunbooks contained the log with the number of rounds fired through the tank's main tube. After firing a certain number of rounds, due to wear and tear, the gun tubes were usually replaced. Thus, gunbooks were a very important maintenance tool for armored vehicles. The Sheridan was a high-maintenance vehicle anyway that was able to fire both conventional 152 mm main gun

rounds and also a rocket propelled missile from the same
main gun tube. I was familiar
with them from my service in
Vietnam with the 11th ACR.
They were also air transportable
and were also assigned to airborne divisions in those days.

As we were looking at the
gunbooks and chatting with
the maintenance officer, Ed
Baltsenberger, a superb captain
who was frustrated by the lack
of support he was getting from
the squadron staff, we noticed
that the entries in the gunbooks did not coincide with
the training history of the unit.
It turned out that the entries in
the gunbooks had been forged
in order to make the gun tubes

Fig. 3 Squadron Command. Left
to right: Unidentified officer,
Chaplain Bernie Leiving, Major
Manosky, LTC Dozier.

seem older than they actually were. Further investigation found that the
turret mechanics had been told to do this by someone in the chain of
command. This was so that the mechanically worn out Sheridans then
could be turned in for rebuild, and the unit would get like-new, recently
renovated vehicles and not have to maintain the old, worn out ones. I
never found out who it was that gave this order.

Gunbooks are like bibles in an Armor unit. When I reported
the problems to our division ordnance unit, it created a firestorm.
USAREUR ordnance sent inspectors to Schwabach to check on our
findings. The USAREUR inspectors were still at Schwabach continuing
to inspect our 27 Sheridans when the 1st Armored Division IG team
arrived to do their annual comprehensive inspection of the entire unit.
After several days, the various inspectors got in the way of each other, and
our soldiers began to question the usefulness of what was going on. They

had worked very hard to get ready for the IG inspection, but things had become disorganized.

Major Manosky, CSM Garofalo and I put our heads together and decided that enough was enough. I told the division IG team to end the inspection, pack up and leave. I really didn't have the authority to do that, but with inspectors inspecting other inspectors and second-guessing each other, it was in the best interest of the unit to do what I did.

I immediately called the division chief of staff, Colonel Jim Aarstad, whom I had known from Vietnam days, and told him what I had done. He reiterated that I had no authority to call off a division level inspection. I explained in detail why I had done what I did. He told me to stand by while he reported all of this to the division CG. I also called my immediate boss, Colonel Byers, who became very upset. At this point I had visions of a very short squadron command tour, and thus the end of my military career.

Colonel Aarstad soon called back and directed me to meet the division CG the next morning at the old division HQ in Göppingen, Germany. So, the next morning CSM Garofalo and I got in a helicopter and flew to meet the CG. I met Colonel Byers in the hall outside of the CG's office, and he told me to be very careful about what I said to the CG. I promised to do so.

When I reported to the CG, MG Jim Galloway, there was an array of the division staff present, including both division DCGs (1-star deputy CGs), Colonel Byers, the chief of staff, the division IG and a few others:

My Reporting to MG Galloway:

Me: "Lieutenant Colonel Dozier reporting as ordered, sir."

MG Galloway did not tell me to stand at ease, sit down or anything else. He left me standing at attention. I vividly remember almost all of the dialogue that followed:

MG Galloway: "I understand that you called off my IG team's inspection of 1-1 Cavalry."

Me: "Yes, sir."

MG Galloway: "Why?"

I explained the whole situation and its background in as few words as possible, then continued:

Me: "Sir, I now know the problems in the unit, but I just need time and resources to fix them."

MG Galloway: "How much time do you need?"

Me: "120 days."

Major Manosky, CSM Garofalo and I had previously discussed this kind of timing, but it was mostly a guess.

MG Galloway: "I'll give you 90 days, then I will send the IG team back. You are dismissed."

Me: "Yes, sir."

I saluted and left.

It is sometimes strange how careers interact. Years later, in 1985, when I was about to retire from active military service, I was interviewed to replace MG Galloway as Commandant of Cadets at Norwich University in Vermont. Two retirement opportunities had opened up at about that time: one at Norwich and the other in my hometown of Arcadia, Florida. I interviewed for the Norwich job in February. I asked MG Patton for advice, since he knew all of the players involved. He told me he would not give me any advice, but he hastened to say that in the town of Northfield, Vermont, if you urinated in your own backyard in the middle of the night, the whole town would be talking about it at breakfast the next morning.

That advice, when coupled with the rigors of New England winters, made it an easy decision. I took the hometown job in Florida and never looked back, even though Arcadia, Florida was a lot like Northfield, a small town where everyone knew everything.

CSM Garofalo and I mapped out a rough plan in the helicopter on the way back to Schwabach. We shared it with Major Manosky, refined it and put it into action. It revolved around centralized planning, team building, goal setting and decentralized execution. Having experienced many IG inspections over the years, the three of us knew what needed to be done. We formed teams in broad functional areas (supply, maintenance, administration, etc.), put an officer, assisted by a strong NCO, in charge of each team, established goals and timelines, then conducted weekly IPRs (In Progress Reviews).

We used a device that I called "The Christmas Tree" to measure progress. It was a large wall chart that listed all of the functional areas of the unit. The Army uses a red, amber and green system to measure readiness: RED, not ready; AMBER, marginally ready, but still needs work; and GREEN, ready. At each weekly IPR, team leaders would rate the functional areas using colored decals that they would stick on the wall chart. Soon, it became festooned with decals of various colors; hence, the nickname Christmas Tree.

It wasn't long before the weekly IPRs engendered competition between those responsible for functional areas. Progress, or lack thereof, was vividly displayed in multicolor for all to see. We were successful. We found that getting ready for the IG inspection became a race that each functional area wanted to win. I would use the Christmas Tree technique numerous times in the future to measure the progress of projects.

When we were re-inspected, we passed each functional area with flying colors, no pun intended. We recognized those responsible at a ceremony in our officers club. In return, the staff presented a color-coded, framed edition of the Christmas Tree to each of us: Major Manosky, CSM Garofalo and me. Needless to say, MG Galloway was pleased. He wrote me a nice letter congratulating us on our success. In addition, the inspection preparation process proved to be a powerful team building endeavor that endured throughout the remainder of my command tour.

We used the same process to rebuild our vehicles that were in bad shape. When I assumed command, about 25% of our vehicles were inoperable. Ed Baltsenberger and his maintenance technician, CWO (Chief Warrant Officer) John Thomas, developed a methodical plan to repair each vehicle. They would prepare a weekly report on the progress. About six months later, we celebrated when 100% of the vehicles in the squadron were combat ready. The same process worked equally as well to prepare our Sheridans (M-551s) and scout vehicles (M-114s), plus their crews for our own gunnery tests.

As I previously mentioned, drugs were a particular problem in most USAREUR units in the early 1970s. The 1-1 Cav was not exempt. We had been working hard, trying to pinpoint which soldiers in the unit were distributing/selling drugs. For instance, we had previously asked the provost marshal to put undercover agents in our unit disguised as transfers from other units. It turned out we were getting close.

One evening, the squadron duty officer, 1LT Don Elder, excitedly called me (I lived nearby on the same kaserne) to tell me that our HQ building had just been firebombed. I quickly dressed and hurried over to the HQ. Luckily, very little damage was done, but Molotov cocktails had been thrown against the windows of my office, the CSM's office and the office of the legal clerk. I called the division provost marshal right away, and he sent an investigating team to Schwabach early the next morning. When they arrived, they asked if I would agree to try out a new investigating technique that had been discussed in various military law enforcement circles. After the investigators explained the plan's details, I readily agreed.

The plan involved assembling the entire 800-man unit, minus the Air Cavalry troop, which was located at Katterbach, 40 miles away from O'Brien Barracks, in the bleachers of our gymnasium. A half dozen interview tables were set up on the gym floor, manned by CID (Criminal Investigation Division) investigators and one of our senior NCOs. The NCOs had a pretty good idea who the drug dealers were, but were having difficulty getting evidence. Most soldiers did not want to be associated with drug users, but were reluctant to inform on them. The provost marshal's plan negated that problem.

Major Manosky, CSM Garofalo and I supervised the entire effort. The plan called for a CID agent to call a soldier, a suspect provided by one of our NCOs, out of the bleachers and down to one of the interview tables. Soon there were interviews going on at each table on the gym floor. From time to time, the CID agents would ask the suspects to turn around while the agent would point in the general direction of a section of the bleachers. The job of the NCO sitting at the table was to watch who was talking to whom in the bleachers or who was acting a little nervous when the agent was pointing. After a soldier was interviewed, he would be segregated from the group in the bleachers. The next interviewee would be selected by the NCO who was watching the group in the bleachers.

The process, which took most of the day, was a clear success. It was liberally interspersed with frequent breaks to go to the bathroom so that soldiers could quietly discuss what was taking place. Pretty soon soldiers felt confident enough to share information with the investigators. Several even confessed to being part of the distribution organization. The investigators were able to build a pretty complete picture of the way drugs were distributed, not only within the 1-1 Cavalry, but also in the surrounding areas as well. We learned, for instance, that a group in nearby Grafenwoehr would supply drugs to the Schwabach area and vice-versa. The dealers and distributors did this in an effort to compartmentalize those involved, as well as from their own operations, thus making detection more difficult.

Our biggest discovery was that our legal clerk, whom we thought to be a good soldier, was the drug kingpin in our squadron. He was beginning to feel threatened by our own internal investigation. He also was the one who had firebombed the offices.

Although this investigation proved to be a setback to the drug operations in the local area, it by no means solved the overall drug problem. Drugs continued to be a major problem in USAREUR until the war in Vietnam wound down and experienced officers and NCOs were reassigned to units in Europe. I remember when we received our first E-8 first sergeant. He turned his unit around in very short time. Leadership is everything.

U.S. Army War College

Toward the end of my tour with the 1-1 Cavalry, I was selected to attend the U.S. Army War College (USAWC), at Carlisle, Pennsylvania, a very important stepping stone in an officer's career. I think I was selected due to the turnaround of the 1-1 Cav. As a result of the turnaround, both Colonel Byers and Major General Galloway wrote very favorable performance appraisals of my command tour.

The course at the USAWC was comparable to a graduate level course (in fact, now, graduates are awarded masters' degrees in strategic studies) and was designed to expand an officer's field of view with regard to where the military fit into the overall national security organization. To me, the year of study was exhilarating and greatly expanded my intellectual horizons. As part of the course, I was in a study group that wrote a paper on Sea-mobile Air Cavalry, a concept to base Army and Marine Air Cavalry units on Navy surface ships. Parts of it were later incorporated into Army, Air Force and Marine Corps doctrine. It provided our military leadership with an alternative to using ground troops and tactical aircraft to secure an area of operations. It was much more precise than a 2,000-pound bomb or an M-1 tank.

We all thoroughly enjoyed the tour. It provided a period of good family time during which my wife, our children and I were reunited with old friends. We were too junior to qualify for on-base housing, so we rented one off-base. Both of our children were attending their second high school, but were doing well. Cheryl again became involved with managing a local high school athletic team, while Scott once again was involved in Little League Baseball and soccer. A number of our friends from previous tours were also attending the course, so it was a lot like "old home week." Little did I realize that some of the new friends I made would be instrumental in subsequent assignments.

One complication during this tour involved my widowed mother (her second husband had just died) coming to live with us. By this time, she had begun to be afflicted with Alzheimer's disease. She enjoyed walking alone several times a day, but would frequently get lost with friends seeing her out and bringing her home. As soon as our Carlisle tour was over, we moved her to Alvin, Texas, where my sister put her into a nursing home. While at Carlisle, we took advantage of frequent opportunities to visit her previously mentioned brother, Bill, who still lived in the Pocono Mountains in northeast Pennsylvania. Since we had a basement fireplace, we took advantage of visits to Uncle Bill to collect some excellent firewood.

In Carlisle, we lived next door to a delightful family. The father, Jay, worked for AMP, an electrical device company in nearby Camp Hill. Jay was a character, but also an expert handyman. We stayed in contact with him and his family for years afterward. One day he called to tell us about a Marine whose ancestors were Polish, who followed us in renting our house. Jay said, "Jim, I have a real live Marine joke." It seems the winter after we moved out was very harsh. The Marine called Jay to tell him that the freezer in the garage was not running. He asked Jay to check it out. Jay did and found that the thermostat in the freezer was set at "0° F" and that the temperature in the garage was 10° F below zero!

Second Pentagon Tour

Following the war college, I was reassigned to the Pentagon. This was somewhat of a surprise, since we had been away for only three years. While at Carlisle, Judy went down to Washington to try to buy our old house back, but we no longer could afford it. Real estate prices had sky-rocketed during those three years we were gone. We finally found a nice house in Vienna, Virginia, but much further from the Pentagon than our old house.

Largely based on my engineering training, I was initially assigned to the Office of the Assistant Secretary of the Army for Research and Development (ASA R&D). I was part of a "Red Team," which was a team led by a civilian, Richard Trainor, whose job was to question all aspects of weapons systems that were then in development. We reported directly to the ASA R&D, Norman Augustine, who was later the CEO of Lockheed Martin.

It was interesting and rewarding work. Dick Trainor purposely selected officers who had recent field experience as members of his team. I was personally responsible for organizing and conducting quarterly Department of the Army Program Reviews (DAPRs) of our major weapons systems. During a DAPR, the Army weapons system program manager would brief selected members of the Army staff on the progress of a given program. A DAPR was an excellent coordination tool for keeping programs on track. Not surprisingly, some of the program managers used the old reliable Christmas Tree chart process to report on the status of their programs.

After about six months in Dick Trainor's office, I was selected for an accelerated promotion to "Full Colonel" (COL). Since I was then "over-ranked" for the job I had, I had to look elsewhere. I told Armor Branch that since we had just purchased a house in nearby Vienna, Virginia, and that the children were just getting settled in high school, we would like to stay in the Washington area.

Shortly after my name appeared on the promotion list, I ran into a war college classmate, Colonel Tom Blagg, in the hall of the Pentagon, who told me that his office, Assistant Secretary of the Army for Financial Management (ASA FM), was reorganizing and was looking for a colonel to fill one of the slots. I checked with Armor Branch and they readily agreed.

I interviewed with Hadley Hull, the assistant secretary, and he gave me the job. It turned out to be one of the best learning experiences I would have. I learned a lot about resource management that would guide me for the remainder of my military career, as well as in future civilian endeavors. My job was to help coordinate, program and budget the Army investment accounts (R&D, Construction, etc.) known as capital accounts in the civilian world. Since I was a member of the Army Secretariat, the civilian staff of the Army, I wore civilian clothes to work.

When our son, Scott, graduated from high school in the summer of 1976, he enlisted in the Coast Guard (Figure 4). Our daughter, Cheryl, had enrolled at Florida State University (FSU) the year before. Quite frankly, we rather enjoyed getting our children "launched," so to speak. We did not suffer an empty nest syndrome, as some do. We were more interested in getting them off and running on their own careers. Scott had not been the best kid in high school (he was into almost everything in which he should not have been), so we marched him down to the Coast

Fig. 4 Scott in the U.S. Coast Guard

Guard recruiters in Alexandria, Virginia and signed him up. A Coast Guard chief petty officer did more to get him sorted out than did Judy or I.

One time in Germany when he was skipping school, we told him, "If we get a good deal on a big dog, son, you're gone. Big dogs are usually trainable, but you are not!" He replied, "If that is the way that you all feel about me, I'm going to run away and stay here in Germany." Judy pointed toward the front door. Scott went upstairs and packed a small suitcase, came back downstairs and started outside. It was raining, so he went back upstairs. He is now an accomplished artist, sculptor and agriculturist.

In late 1976, after two years in the two jobs in the Pentagon, I was selected for brigade command. Each year, in addition to convening promotion boards, the Army convenes a board to select colonels (paygrade O-6) for brigade command, a very necessary step for further advancement.

First Fort Hood Tour—Brigade Command

As soon as the colonels' command list came out, Major General Patton, then commanding general of the 2nd Armored Division (2AD) at Fort Hood, Texas, persuaded Armor Branch to assign me to his division, again, mentorship at work. MG Patton slated me to command the 2nd (St. Lo) Brigade (Figure 5), which was having some problems. During WWII, the 2nd Brigade led the breakout of the Normandy bridgehead through the town of Saint-Lô, France, thus acquiring the nickname.

Fig. 5 - 2nd Brigade
WWII M-4 tank

When I arrived at Fort Hood, the current brigade commander had not yet finished his command tour, so I was assigned to III Corps HQ to help develop the plans for a corps-wide map exercise that would take place later that year. A corps is the next larger tactical organization than a division. At that time at Fort Hood, we had two divisions, 1st Cavalry and the 2nd Armored, both heavy divisions with a large number of tanks and armored personnel carriers. In addition, there were corps support units also assigned: a signal brigade, a military police brigade, a military intelligence brigade, an engineer brigade, an air cavalry brigade and numerous smaller units that support an installation of about 45,000 soldiers, plus their families.

At such a large installation at Fort Hood, there also was the office of the deputy post commander, who was in charge of all the installation housekeeping. Of course, the corps CG, assisted by his tactical and installation staffs, was responsible for the activities of the entire installation. III Corp's wartime mission at that time was to reinforce NATO in the event of war with the Warsaw Pact. In order to do so, we frequently conducted corps-level exercises of one form or another.

I reported directly to Major General John Hill, the deputy corps commander. The corps commander at that time was Lieutenant General Robert Shoemaker. I headed a team of six to eight officers that started to put the map exercise together. We made fairly rapid progress and again used the "Christmas Tree" to measure our completion of tasks.

Fig. 6 Jim as Brigade Commander

Fig. 7 - 2nd Brigade HQ

After several months working at III Corps HQ, I assumed command of the 2nd Brigade (Figure 6 and Figure 7). MG Patton had previously discussed with me various issues that I needed to take a look at within the brigade. Some involved the subordinate battalions (there were four: two armored and two infantry). Other issues revolved around the organization of the brigade HQ itself. He told me that he would assign a new brigade executive officer (XO), who was highly recommended by a classmate, Doc Bahnsen, with whom we had both served in Vietnam. LTC Richard Sklar arrived at the 2nd Brigade and we both went to work. Dick Sklar was a superb organizer, perfect as an XO.

The primary mission of the brigade was to train rotational battalions for duty with a sister brigade (4th Brigade) in Northern Germany. We would rotate battalions every six months, but training for rotation, which involved a great deal of field training, would take nearly a year. The units had to be combat ready when they were assigned to NATO. Once we finished our stint of training a Europe-bound unit, the task was

Fig. 8 – 2nd Brigade briefing

handed off to another brigade. We, then, were given a new mission: participating in what came to be known as the Division Restructuring Study tests (DRS tests). The DRS tests were the highlight of my 2nd Brigade command tour: the maneuver of brigade-sized units in force-on-force engagements.

The objective of the DRS tests was to determine if the Army should restructure armor and mechanized infantry battalions of the heavy force. The tests involved pitting a currently organized heavy force brigade against a brigade with a different organizational structure. The 2AD supplied the currently organized brigade (2nd Brigade, which I commanded). The 1st Cavalry Division supplied the variably organized brigade (commanded by Colonel John Foss, a classmate).

During the DRS maneuvers, each of the major vehicles, as well as some individual soldiers, were equipped with a laser hit/kill device that would indicate if the shooter had achieved a kill. For instance, if a tank gunner successfully engaged another tank, the target tank's laser receptor would automatically activate a blinking light and a smoke grenade. When that occurred, the tank driver was trained to stop the target tank in place. The same was true for individual soldiers who had been successfully engaged—the laser receptor would turn on a blinking light and the soldier was required to remain in place.

We tested various day and night offensive and defensive scenarios against each other, always using the same terrain, in an effort to minimize the variables involved. We then briefed the results (Figure 8). We ran scenarios that pitted both forces against a simulated Warsaw Pact heavy brigade. The results of the tests showed that the currently organized brigade, with some tweaking, was more robust than most of the experimental formations. The tests were a superb training experience for all of us who were involved. They gave us total confidence in our equipment, our doctrine, our organization and our training.

Also, while a brigade commander at Fort Hood, I joined a task force that helped rebuild force structure and doctrine after the Vietnam War. This effort later paid tremendous dividends during the two invasions of Iraq.

During this period, I found out that MG Patton was an ardent fisherman, as were some of his key commanders. Since I had a boat and also enjoyed fishing, early on during my brigade command tour I was welcomed into the Saturday morning bass fishing tournament. There were usually five to six boats competing. We would fish the local lakes, usually Lake Belton and Stillhouse Reservoir. On occasion, we would take a long weekend and fish some of the other lakes in Texas. I was usually teamed with Glenn Finkbiner, an old friend from previous tours (Germany and Vietnam).

A usual morning on a local lake would begin with MG Patton launching his boat with the help of his 11- to 12-year old son Ben. MG Patton could not back a boat trailer very well, so he had a trailer hitch put on the front of his pickup truck. He would put Ben in the boat and begin his assault on the boat ramp. It took numerous tries, all the while hollering at Ben to do this, do that, in order to get his boat in the water. After he and Ben had their boat in the water and had begun stowing their fishing gear, the rest of us would launch our boats. It was a great and often humorous way to start a Saturday morning.

Toward the end of my 18-month command tour with the 2nd Brigade, MG Patton was succeeded in command of the 2AD by MG Charles P. Graham, a friend of mine from a previous European tour. When I commanded the 1-1 Cav in Schwabach, MG Graham, then a colonel, commanded the 2ACR in nearby Nuremberg. As previously mentioned, his and my daughter, Susan and Cheryl, both attended Nuremberg High School. Frequently, when there was an after school event, Cheryl would spend the night with Susan at the Grahams, rather than ride the bus home to Schwabach. In addition, when the 2ACR went to a training area as a regiment, the 1-1 Cav would replace them on the East-West German border, and at various times we would be attached to the 2ACR during maneuvers.

When I relinquished command of the 2nd Brigade, the change of command ceremony was a very memorable occasion. My successor passed out on the reviewing stand just as the ceremony began! Initially, my successor, MG Graham and I were all standing together on the reviewing stand at the division parade ground (Figure 9). We heard a thump! My successor had collapsed. By this time, the troops had formed on the parade field and the ceremony was underway. MG Graham looked at me with sort of a "what do we do now?" look. I told him that we would just play things by ear.

As the brigade executive officer brought the brigade colors forward, MG Graham and I dismounted from the reviewing stand and took our positions to transfer the colors. Normal procedure for transferring the brigade colors to the new commander would have involved the brigade command sergeant major (BCSM) taking the colors from the color guard, and then passing them on to the commander, who was departing. He then would hand them to MG Graham. MG Graham would then hand them to the incoming commander, who would hand them back to the BCSM, who would return them to the color guard (Figure 9).

We followed the normal procedure to the point at which MG Graham would hand the colors to the new commander. When MG Graham received the colors from me, I told the brigade executive officer, who had brought the color guard forward, to step forward to receive the colors. He had been watching what had transpired on the reviewing stand and had expected a change in the normal procedure. He received the colors, returned them to the BCSM, who returned them to the color guard. All was well.

MG Graham and I returned to the reviewing stand, made some brief remarks, and after the troops had passed in review, we were briefed on what had occurred with the incoming commander. It turned out that medics immediately attended to him after he collapsed and discovered

Fig. 9 Brigade change of command

that he was infected with a virus. He quickly recovered and the virus was not transferred to us.

Chief of Staff Tours

Shortly after he arrived at the 2AD, MG Graham asked me if I would agree to remain at Fort Hood to be the chief of staff (C/S) of the 2AD when I finished my command tour. I readily agreed, in that being a division C/S was a choice assignment. It also was a career broadening experience for me. The position involved coordinating the various staff agencies of a very large armored division (four brigades) that had units not only at Fort Hood, but also one with a forward deployed brigade in Europe. A C/S was responsible for doing what the name implies: coordinating all of the divisional staff activities, regardless of where those brigades were.

After less than a year as C/S of 2AD, LTG Marvin (Red) Fuller replaced LTG Robert Shoemaker as CG of III Corps and Fort Hood. LTG Fuller had recently been the inspector general of the Army. The entire Army at that time was rebuilding and reorganizing itself in the wake of ending the U.S. involvement in Vietnam. The DRS tests, previously mentioned, were part of this effort. LTG Shoemaker had begun the process, but was selected for his fourth star and command of Forces Command (FORCECOM) in Atlanta, Georgia. LTG Fuller's task was to complete the job. In addition to an emphasis on training, LTG Fuller focused attention on resource management. This was a major task. The total population of Fort Hood was over 45,000 military, and nearly as many civilian workers and dependents, thus constituting a huge command and installation.

One of the things LTG Fuller did was to decentralize budget formulation and execution down to the battalion level. Each major unit, from battalion on up, was required to keep accurate records of training and operational costs. The process would begin with each unit developing an annual training program, then costing it using standard metrics provided by the Department of the Army. Each unit next would form a Program and Budget Advisory Committee (PBAC), which would meet periodically to review progress. This committee was an excellent tool in managing resources.

As C/S of the 2AD, I was responsible for organizing and conducting the periodic PBAC reviews at the division level. During the time MG Graham was in command, I would also attend the PBAC reviews at III Corps, conducted by my classmate Colonel Dave Palmer, the Corps G-3 (Operations and Training) officer. I modeled 2AD PBAC reviews along the same lines as those of III Corps, so that we fit seamlessly in the process.

LTG Fuller was also a "hands-on" CG, much to the consternation of the commanders of the corps units, especially the two division commanders who felt that he was intruding onto their turf. Initially, I had the same feeling. For instance, I would get to the office at about 6:30 a.m., each morning. One of my first tasks, if the division duty officer had not called me during the night, was to check the military police blotter for incidents that had occurred, so that I could brief MG Graham on them when he arrived, usually shortly after I did.

On several occasions, when I arrived at 2AD HQ in the morning, the duty officer would tell me that LTG Fuller was waiting for me in my office. When I asked why I was not called, the answer always would be that LTG Fuller had told the duty officer not to call. Sure enough, I would find LTG Fuller sitting in a chair in my office reading a magazine, patiently waiting for me to arrive. He would then ask about certain items on the MP blotter, after which we would chat about various events going on at Fort Hood.

If I had been called by the duty officer, I was usually fully conversant on the night's events. If I had not been called, I would tell him that I was not aware of that particular incident, but would look into it right away. That seemed to satisfy him. He would usually tell me to make sure that MG Graham was aware of the event and he then asked me to ask MG Graham to give him a call. Having the corps CG get to my office before I did was intimidating to me, but it also infuriated MG Graham. I checked with the C/S of the other division on the post to see if the same thing was happening there. It was.

It turns out that in addition to letting subordinate commanders know that he was interested in what soldiers were doing off duty, LTG Fuller was shopping for a new corps C/S. His current C/S, Colonel Johnny Johnston, had just been selected as a brigadier general and needed to be replaced.

One morning MG Graham rushed into my office to tell me that "Red Fuller just called to tell me that he has selected you to be his next chief of staff." MG Graham was very upset and so was I. This was a bolt out of the blue; a complete surprise. I enjoyed being a division C/S; however, I had reservations about working for LTG Fuller. He had intimidated me by showing up in my office early in the morning and he had been tough on division CGs.

After I had thought about the job change for a while, I called Judy and told her what was about to happen and that we might think about retiring from the Army. I went on to say that I wasn't sure that I could work well with a man who intimidated me. Judy had gotten to know LTG Fuller socially pretty well. He was sort of an introvert. During social functions at his quarters, he usually did not participate in general conversations. Instead, he would stand by the fireplace with a drink in his hand and just watch what was taking place. His wife, on the other hand, was a delightful lady, who was also a gracious host. Judy told me she would go along with whatever decision I made, but that I should think long and hard about leaving the Army. I did just that and decided to take the job.

It turned out I had completely misjudged LTG Fuller. After about six weeks on the job, I was his biggest fan. He had already gone a long way toward rebuilding, reorganizing and retraining III Corps, but the job was not yet done and he was losing his very strong, current C/S. He explained to me that he wanted me to pick up where Colonel Johnston had left off. He further explained the difficulties he was facing and told me that after looking over the corps, he felt sure I was the man to help finish the job. I thanked him for his confidence in me and went to work. We were a good team and he was very instrumental in furthering my career.

CHAPTER 6

Promotion to General Officer

In late 1979 LTG Fuller was a member of the brigadier general selection board that selected me for brigadier general (BG). He joined MG Patton as being one of the most influential persons in my military career, a true mentor.

As a BG selectee, I attended a session in Washington with other selectees, where the Army chief of staff briefed us regarding what he expected of general officers. In addition, he told us that we would all attend a two-week course at the Center for Creative Leadership (CCL) in Greensboro, North Carolina, with civilians as well as military. This course would give us a look at ourselves through the eyes of others. He emphasized that what we see in the mirror each morning is usually not what others see. He hit the nail right on the head. The course was also designed to help a newly selected flag officer get his feet back on the ground.

What I learned at CCL during those two weeks stood me in good stead for the rest of my military career, as well as in civilian life after retirement. I have recommended attendance to several new civilian CEOs, who subsequently attended the course.

When we first got to CCL, we were broken into small groups of about 10 people each and given the name of a person in the group to pay special attention to during the two weeks. We were also told that at the end of the course, we would, in groups, give reports on our observations of the person whose name we were given. In addition, we were asked to tell the group what we had gotten out of the course.

By the end of the two weeks, we were so thoroughly analyzed by the faculty that we had no compunctions talking about what we had seen in others, or about our own deficiencies.

At the end of our course group session, one of our members spoke about what she had gotten out of the course. She was the wife of a Hershey Foods executive who had previously attended the course and who insisted that his wife also attend. This was because they were having marriage difficulties.

She was very succinct. She said, "The main thing that I have gotten out of the course is that the problem in our marriage is me." The members of our group stayed in contact with each other for a number of years. This woman and her husband now have a very stable marriage.

In early 1980, I received my promotion to brigadier general, but learned that my first assignment would be to a position that would provide multi-service or allied operational experience. Up until this point, almost all of my assignments had been Army oriented. The U.S. military wanted its generals and admirals to be as well rounded as possible, so service with other branches of the U.S. military (joint service) and with foreign militaries (combined service) was usually a prerequisite for promotion. Until then, I had not served with any other branch of the U.S. military, and other than meeting NATO officials, I had no combined service. This was about to change.

The General Officer Management Office (GOMO) quickly told me that I would be assigned to a position on a NATO staff in Verona, Italy. I was being assigned to the Land Component (LANDSOUTH) of the Allied Forces Southern Europe (AFSOUTH), and would be sent to the Defense Language Institute (DLI) in Monterey, California, to learn Italian. I was given less than a week to pack up our household goods and head for California. I didn't even have written orders; I was told they would be waiting for me as we passed through Fort Bliss, Texas, on our way to California. This was my first experience with the general officer assignment branch. I would soon learn that these assignments are often not as orderly as those of others in the rest of the Army.

At the last minute, Cheryl, who had been working in the U.K. after graduating from Florida State University (FSU), joined us for the trip to California. We drove three cars, connected by CB radios: Judy drove our 1969 Volkswagen Beetle; Cheryl, our 1973 Ford Pinto station wagon; and I brought up the rear in our 1980 Oldsmobile, pulling a boat. We arrived at the Presidio of Monterey, largely without incident. The CB radios kept us in contact when we became separated. I picked up my movement orders, as planned, at Fort Bliss on the way out.

When we arrived at DLI, Cheryl was unexpectedly allowed to attend the Italian language course with Judy and me, so she decided to spend the rest of the time at Monterey with us. That decision had a profound effect on her future career. When she graduated from FSU with a master's degree in medical social work, she intended to work in that field. When she was about to finish high school, she was offered several scholarships, including an Army ROTC scholarship. I encouraged her to accept it, but she said, "Dad, I have been in the Army for 18 years and I think that is enough."

While at DLI, Cheryl met several junior U.S. Air Force (USAF) officers, who convinced her that maybe a military career would be right down her alley. Much to my wife's and my surprise, one day during the course she announced that she would like to join the Air Force. We were delighted. During DLI we hooked her up with a recruiter and finalized her paperwork at Randolph AFB, Texas, on our way back to the East Coast. She attended Officer Candidate School at Lackland AFB, Texas, and, since I was already in Italy, was commissioned by one of my classmates, BG Doc Bahnsen, the same Doc Bahnsen with

Fig. 1 Colonel Cheryl Dozier, USAF (Ret)

whom I served in the 11th ACR in Vietnam, who was then stationed at nearby Fort Hood, Texas. Cheryl (Figure 1) retired 26 years later as a full colonel (O-6), after a distinguished Air Force career.

The tour at DLI had its more enjoyable and lighter moments. The Monterey Peninsula is a beautiful part of America. There were numerous superb restaurants in the immediate area, as well as stunning scenery. The

tour also allowed us to reconnect with
Glenn and Sylvia Finkbiner (Figure 2),
friends from earlier tours.

Fig. 2 Glenn and
Sylvia Finkbiner

Glenn and I were ardent fishermen
and Monterey Bay turned out to be
a fisherman's paradise. Each Saturday
morning, we would meet at the Monterey Coast Guard Station small boat
launching ramp, put my boat in the
water, and fish.

One morning I was up front steering the boat, with Glenn in the rear
when I heard him yell, "Jesus Christ, keep the engine running so they
will know where we are." I looked back and saw a plume of water squirt
into the air, then a gray back break the surface. We were in a herd of gray
whales that reach lengths of 40–49 feet, much larger than my 16-foot
boat. However, they never bothered us. We encountered these whales
several more times during the next couple of weeks. Monterey Bay is on
their migration route from Alaska to Mexico.

Learning a language was hard work for me. I was sort of a linguistic
klutz. Italian was difficult for Judy also. It was a breeze for Cheryl, and
she became rather fluent in Italian. Judy and I learned enough to get by.
Later, I would learn a lot more from my Italian driver, DiNardo, than I
ever did at DLI. Even though DiNardo spoke very little English, he had
been the driver for my predecessor, BG Larry Wright, who as an LTC
had been XO of the 11th ACR when I first reported to the regiment
in Vietnam. DiNardo was a member of the Carabinieri, a paramilitary
police force. It provided law enforcement functions for both the Italian
military, as well as for Italy at large. Almost any town of a reasonable size,
even in the middle of nowhere, had a Carabinieri station located in it.

Italy Tour

Verona is a beautiful northern Italian city located in the southern foot-
hills of the Alps (Figure 3). On a clear day, we could see the snow-capped
Alps from our penthouse patio. We lived in a lovely apartment (Figure
4), on the top floor and penthouse of a seven-story high-rise building in
Verona, the setting for Shakespeare's Romeo and Juliet.

One of my jobs was to act as a point of contact (POC) for many of the dealings with AFSOUTH, which was primarily a U.S. headquarters, whose commander-in-chief (CINC) was Admiral William Crowe. As a result, I traveled frequently between Verona and Naples to attend meetings and other briefings. I also attended quarterly coordination meetings at the U.S. Embassy in Rome. All of the trips between Verona and Rome and Naples were made by car. I was assigned a NATO sedan, an Alfa Romeo nicknamed by DiNardo as La Dodici (the Italian word for "twelve") since its NATO license plate number was 12. These trips were a linguistic, total immersion as we would spend hours together in the sedan driving around Italy. I also learned a lot about the culture of Italy from him.

My assignment at LAND-SOUTH was as the Deputy Chief of Staff for Administration and Logistics. It was a position occupied by an

Fig. 3 Italy map

Fig. 4 Dozier apartment building

American general for many years. LANDSOUTH was a predominantly Italian HQ, but members of all the NATO nations were represented. The commander-in-chief (CINC) of the HQ was initially General

Santini (Figure 5). He was a seasoned officer who was imprisoned and mistreated
by the Nazis when Italy surrendered in
1943. He spoke fluent English and he and
his staff worked well with the rest of the
AFSOUTH.

Fig. 5 General Santini

Since I was the senior American officer
assigned to LANDSOUTH, I had a small
staff that supported me, as well as the
other Americans (about a dozen) assigned
to the HQ. For strictly U.S. military business, mostly personnel-oriented, I worked
directly with the U.S. element at NATO
HQ in Mons, Belgium.

A large American military base was
located at Vicenza, about an hour east of Verona. Vicenza was home
to two good-sized military organizations: SETAF (Southern European
Task Force), an American HQ located at Caserma Ederle, and 5ATAF
(5th Allied Tactical Air Force), the air element of AFSOUTH, located
at nearby Dal Molin Air Base. SETAF was commanded by Major General William McFadden. An Italian general commanded 5ATAF, with
an American general as his deputy. SETAF's mission included logistic
support for U.S. units in the Mediterranean region. It also included the
173rd Airborne Brigade, a quick reaction force for the same area. I also
relied on the SETAF intelligence staff section, led by Lieutenant Colonel
Bill Reed, for "U.S. eyes only" intelligence. Vicenza also housed a U.S.
military commissary, a hospital, a post exchange and an American K-12
school.

In addition to my military duties, I was also the community leader
of the small group of Americans in Verona. These members were, in
addition to those assigned to LANDSOUTH, mostly USAF commu-
nicators assigned to communications sites in the southern Italian Alps.
As community leader, I was responsible for the support of all American
service personnel and their families living in the Verona area, regardless of branch of service. To do this, I maintained an "American Affairs
Office" that provided administrative support (passports, ID Cards, Red

Cross support personnel actions), among other tasks. To coordinate our efforts, we interacted with the U.S. Embassy in Rome and with the various branches of the U.S. armed forces stationed in other parts of Europe. We also had an American elementary school in Verona. Middle and high schoolers were bused to the base at Vicenza, about an hour away. In addition, we had a contracted Protestant missionary who conducted Sunday services at the elementary school. Catholics usually went to a local Catholic church.

Judy and I enjoyed life in Italy. My military duties were not overly demanding, so we had plenty of time to get to know the country. On weekends, we would usually drive around the countryside, visiting historical sites. We had plenty of visits from friends who were stationed in other parts of Europe. In particular, many of our friends came from West Germany, where most Americans in Europe were stationed at that time. Since we were in one of the most celebrated wine regions (Soave and Valpolicella) in Italy, we would often visit small wineries. These wineries would allow customers to taste their vintages right out of wooden casks or large jugs. If you liked a wine, they would bottle it for you right on the spot. We assembled quite a collection. From time to time, we would also visit friends in Germany. However, times were about to change for us in Italy. They had already changed for many Americans in Central Europe.

By 1981, at the height of the Cold War, NATO and the Warsaw Pact were arrayed against each other. Both sides possessed large conventional and nuclear land, sea and air forces that were always on heightened alert. In Western Europe, a number of left-wing terrorist groups had formed that were upset with NATO in general and the U.S. in particular. Initially, they acted rather independently, organizing protests and demonstrations. National government law enforcement agencies at the time were able to more or less contain them. Italy had its Red Brigades; in France there was Direct Action; and Germany faced the Red Army Faction (formerly the Baader-Meinhof Gang). In the early 1970s, these groups became more violent, assassinating public officials in various NATO countries. Almost every NATO country had some left-wing organization causing trouble.

However, the game was about to change. During the late 1970s, the Soviet Union deployed SS-20 missiles in Warsaw Pact countries. NATO responded with a plan to deploy cruise missiles in the U.K., West Germany, the Netherlands, Belgium and Italy. Left-wing organizations then erupted in an attempt to block cruise missile deployments. The Soviet Union saw an opportunity with these groups and started to resource them politically with funding and organizers, as well as with weapons and explosives.

For instance, I later learned that one of the women in the Red Brigades, Emanuela Frascella, the daughter of a prominent Italian medical doctor, who rented the apartment in which I would be held after I was kidnapped, would periodically use her dad's yacht, moored near Venice. Occasionally, she would go out onto the Adriatic Sea to meet arms supply vessels originating in Lebanon and Syria. The weapons and supplies would be off-loaded to her yacht and then brought ashore in Italy. The Soviets themselves would seldom get directly involved. Usually, they would act through proxies such as East Germany and other Warsaw Pact states. Once these indigenous terrorist groups had access to additional resources, they became much more effective. With Warsaw Pact assistance, they began to coordinate their activities and became a much more difficult law enforcement problem throughout Europe.

By the time I got to Italy, left-wing activity was starting to peak. It was mostly concentrated in Central Europe, although in Italy the Red Brigades had assassinated Aldo Moro, the Italian prime minister. The Red Brigades directed most of their activities against Italian politicians, industrialists, journalists, judges and police. We on Italian NATO assignments didn't feel directly threatened. That, too, was about to change.

In West Germany, the Red Army Faction (RAF) set off bombs at the entrance to the USAF Europe HQ at Ramstein AFB. They also bombed the officers' club and rail yard at Rhein Main AFB, near Frankfurt. They made an attempt to kill the CINC of U.S. Army Europe, General Kroesen and his wife, by firing rocket propelled grenades (RPGs) at a sedan in which they were passengers. Fortunately, they escaped serious injury.

In Italy, we were of course aware of these events, but our intelligence did not indicate a threat to us in this part of NATO. We were lulled into somewhat of a false sense of security.

CHAPTER 7

Kidnapping

I was kidnapped on December 17, 1981, as part of a Red Brigades effort to bring down the then current Italian government. Previously, Italy, as a member of NATO, had agreed to the installation of cruise missiles in Sicily. As mentioned in the previous chapter, others were to be installed in the Netherlands, Belgium, the U.K. and West Germany. The installation of cruise missiles was in response to an SS-20 missile deployment threat posed by the Warsaw Pact. Left-wing groups all over Western Europe erupted in response to the NATO decision with bombings, assassinations and attacks on infrastructure.

For instance, a military sedan car-rying General Kroesen, the senior U.S. Army officer in Europe, and his wife, was attacked by RPGs fired by the Red Army Faction (RAF), an outgrowth of the infamous Baader-Meinhof Gang (Figure 1). The RAF also initiated a series of bombings at Rhein Main AFB, the U.S. gateway from the air to Europe (Figure 2). The RAF in addition set off a bomb

Fig. 1 General Kroesen's battered sedan (Stars and Stripes)

in front of USAFE headquarters at Ramstein AFB, injuring
a number of people. Direct
Action, a French left-wing
group, assassinated LTC Ray,
an assistant Army attaché, as
he was going to work one
morning. There were numerous other attacks in Greece
and Turkey.

Fig. 2 Baader-Meinhof Bombing
at Rhein Main AFB

Similar violence in Italy
began in the mid-70s. The
Red Brigades put together a campaign plan named "The Winter of Fire,"
designed to bring down the current Italian government. It was their hope
that the succeeding government would not allow the cruise missiles to
be installed. It was a comprehensive plan that included, in addition to
kidnappings and assassination of key officials, the shooting down of civilian airliners with shoulder fired surface-to-air missiles (SAMs) at major
airports.

Also, as part of that plan, they wanted to kidnap/assassinate a senior
American officer. The Red Brigades were upset with NATO, as well as
America. They considered going after one of the many senior officers
at the AFSOUTH headquarters in Naples, Italy. However, they found
that the security there was pretty tight and they didn't have a very good
organization in that area.

Instead, they decided to go north for about the same reasons they
rejected the south: they were better organized up north and the security
in northern Italy was not as tight as down south. There were three American general officers in northern Italy: two (one Army, one USAF) at
Vicenza and one Army (me) at Verona. For security and organizational
reasons, they decided to go after me. Since they were against NATO in
general and Americans in particular, I was the perfect fit; an American
general in a NATO headquarters.

The Details of the Kidnapping

I arrived home (Figure 3) early from work at the NATO HQ LAND-SOUTH on December 17, 1981, in order to get ready for a Verona Community Council meeting of our small American community. Verona is a lovely, historic town in northern Italy.

Fig. 3 Dozier apartment building

Judy and I were having a drink in the kitchen of our seventh-floor apartment when the doorbell at our apartment door rang. That was somewhat unusual, because in a building such as ours, there were two doorbell systems: one was operated from the front door of the building itself (Figure 4). This system lets a person who wants to contact someone in the building press a button opposite the person's name to be contacted, which activates an intercom in the designated apartment. The person in the apartment then can either open the front door electrically or tell them to go away.

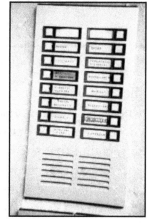

Fig. 4 Street-level doorbells

This doorbell had not rung and Judy was a little concerned about it. I told her not to worry. Famous last words. I went to the front door and asked who was there. The answer came back that they were plumbers and there was a water leak in the apartment downstairs. They wanted to check our apartment to see if that was where the water was coming from. It sounded reasonable to me. The building was about 20 years old and things were always going wrong somewhere.

Figure 5 is a schematic of the first floor of our apartment. On the far right is a den. On the far left is a washroom and utility room. The main entrance, where the doorbell was, is in the center. These are the areas in the apartment where most of the activity was about to take place. I opened the front door and there stood two young men who looked like plumbers and who acted like plumbers, so I let them in. I figured that

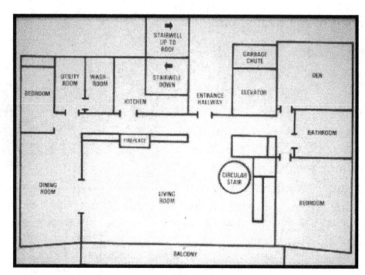

Fig. 5 Dozier apartment diagram

the most likely spot for a leak would be our washroom and utility room, where the washing machine, dryer and sink were located. We checked the area for leaks, but couldn't find any. About that time Judy joined us to mention that she had used the washing machine that day. Her presence seemed to surprise the two men. They then asked me questions about other possibilities for leaks, using several Italian words that I didn't understand. I told them that we had better go back to the kitchen where I keep an Italian-English dictionary so I could figure out what they were talking about.

We went back to the kitchen. Judy started fixing dinner again while I was looking up the words in the dictionary. That's when the fight started.

I was jumped from the rear, spun around and was looking down the barrels of two silenced pistols. Judy immediately dropped to her knees. A fight started that I rapidly began to lose. Finally, I was hit by a fist to the left side of my head and I went down on my back in the hallway outside the kitchen. When I looked back into the kitchen, one of the two young men who had rushed past me and the person I was scuffling with, now had Judy on her knees with a pistol pointed at her head. In English, he said to her, "Shut up or we will kill your husband!" That's when the fight was over. I told Judy to do as they say. If looks could have killed, I would have been dead right then. It turns out that Judy had told me the

Fig. 6 Judy's chains

Fig. 7 Packing case

same thing while I was busy with the other guy and I didn't hear her. She has always accused me of selective listening.

I was immediately handcuffed, blindfolded and gagged. The men let two more individuals into the apartment, who immediately began to ransack it.

Judy was immobilized with chains (Figure 6). They chained her wrists behind her back, then chained her ankles together and ran another chain between the wrist chain and ankle chain to completely immobilize her. They then dragged her to a corner of the kitchen while they dealt with me.

Fig. 8 Jim's body trunk

They brought the packing case (Figure 7) into the hallway outside of the kitchen. Externally, it looked like a packing carton for a small refrigerator. It was padded on the inside, but from my standpoint, it had one major design flaw: no air holes. When one was in the box and the lid closed, a serious problem presented itself. Some of our neighbors saw the case both come into and leave the apartment. They had no idea that a kidnapping was taking place.

I was loaded into what I now will call a trunk (Figure 8) and taken downstairs in the building elevator to a courtyard behind the apartment building. There it was loaded into what I later found out to be a rented van. I was then driven across the

Fig. 9 Padova apartment building

Adige River to the basement parking garage of another high-rise apartment building, where the box was transferred to the back of, once again what I later found out, was a Fiat hatchback. We then traveled, using back roads, for about an hour and a half to Padova, another very lovely town in northeastern Italy. As we traveled along the back roads, the terrorists would close the lid as we went through a town, but would immediately open it again to check my pulse and breathing as we cleared a town.

My sense of smell gave me clues from time to time regarding who was in the car and where we were headed. The person who would open and close the box appeared to be a female. I could smell her perfume. Being able to smell also gave me a clue as to where we were heading. As we traveled, I could smell a bakery in one town and an oil refinery in another. I knew that there were two roads leading away from Verona with large bakeries and oil refineries. One led south to Modena; the eastern road led toward Venice and Padova.

Once we got to Padova, I was brought to another high-rise apartment building (Figure 9), specifically into a second-floor apartment that looked over the parking lot of a supermarket. The box was taken out of the hatchback and put into the building elevator, which they ran up and down several times to disorient me.

We finally stopped on the second floor. I was taken inside an apartment and dumped on a bunk which was inside a tent set up inside one of the

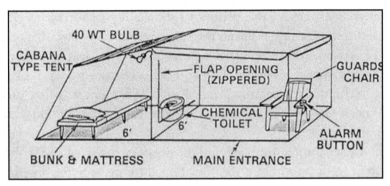

Fig. 10 Dozier holding tent

rooms (Figure 10). The metal bunk had a pillow and mattress. In addition, there was a chemical toilet and a light bulb. They would change the bulb from blue to white at times to disorient me with regard to time. I was chained to the bunk by my arm and a leg, one chain around my wrist, another around my ankle. At no time was I not chained to the bunk. I was also forced to wear earphones, through which recorded music was played 24 hours a day.

I was generally well treated. I was fed three meals a day and the wounds I had suffered in the fight back in Verona, a cracked sinus and ruptured ear drum, were treated with pills that I was told were antibiotics. They also provided an ear ointment. Three men and one woman rotated guard duty, sitting on a chair in the outer portion of the tent. I had had no training on how to handle a situation like this, so I relied on instinct, common sense and a little dumb luck. It turns out that I did a couple of things that enhanced my chances of survival.

When I was first thrown on the bunk (Figure 11), the kidnappers were celebrating their success by high-fiving each other and waving loaded pistols around. Each time I would make the slightest move, they would react violently and pin me down on the bunk. I thought that this was not good. After that brief introduction, I decided to

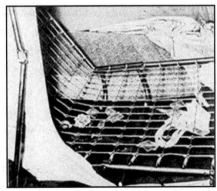

Fig. 11 Cot inside tent

make myself a more reliable prisoner. I did so by structuring my time so that I did the same thing during the same period every day. This paid off, as I will explain. After the initial evening and once I was secured to the bunk, the guards were never armed and they always wore ski masks.

This technique of erecting a tent inside of a room was first used by Argentinean terrorists in the early 1970s. It was designed to do a couple of things:

First, by separating the guard and the prisoner, in this case with the flap of the tent (return to Figure 10), they hoped to preclude the onset of the Stockholm syndrome: a relationship that sometimes develops between a guard and a prisoner held in close proximity to each other for extended periods of time. Patty Hearst is an example of how that might work. In my case, it turns out that one of the guards was somewhat affected by the syndrome, which worked to my benefit when I was rescued, as I will explain later in this chapter.

The second thing it is designed to do is to allow the guards to completely control the environment in which they were holding a prisoner. They were completely successful in this respect for about the first week. None of my senses could penetrate the walls of the tent. After about a week, due to the structuring of my day, the guards did not watch me as closely as they had been. On occasions when the guard was not watching, I could sneak the earphones off. One of the first things I heard was vehicular traffic outside of the building. I could hear the morning and evening buildup of traffic. This allowed me to tell time. It also indicated that I was in an urban area, not at some location far out in the country. By being able to tell time, I was able to keep a diary. At the end of the 42 days, I was two days off. I think I lost those two days during the early period when they were switching the light bulb from blue to white.

Early on, I asked for and was given playing cards and reading material. The reading material consisted of the foreign editions of *Time* and *Newsweek*, plus some Italian news magazines and English language novels. I played a lot of Solitaire. This intrigued the guards, who were not familiar with the game. When they asked about it, I would explain as best I could. Initially, I would keep score by scratching the scores, with my fingernail, onto a corrugated box top that I kept under the bunk. After watching me do this for a day or two, one of the guards brought me some paper and the stub of a pencil. That gave me the idea of keeping a diary.

I developed a base seven alpha-numeric code that I embedded into the Solitaire scores, using the seven piles of cards used in Solitaire and the number of cards in each pile. I figured that if need be, I could explain to the guards what I was doing, based upon my previous attempt to explain the game to them. It turns out they never showed any additional interest.

From the *Time* and *Newsweek* magazines, I got a feel for the international interest in the kidnapping. The guards would tear out the articles dealing with the kidnapping, but they would forget to tear out the table of contents. So, from titles in the table of contents such as "Massive Manhunt in Italy," I knew that the kidnapping was attracting major international attention. Also, from the Italian news magazines, I was able to get a feel for the general area of where I was. Some of the ads in the magazines were from businesses in the Veneto region of northeast Italy. That, coupled with the smells noted during the ride to Padova, made me pretty sure that I was somewhere near Venice and Padova.

The "Peoples' Court" Trial

I was told that I was in a "Peoples' Prison" and that I would be put on trial as a war criminal. The trial began with questioning by Antonio Savasta (Figure 12), a member of the Red Brigades Executive Committee and chief of the Veneto Column. He was accompanied by one other person. He and the other person would come into my portion of the tent and sit on the floor. I would sit on the bunk. Savasta would read a list questions from a ruled pad. Each session was recorded. I told them at the start that I would not answer any questions I considered to be of a classified nature, but would tell them the truth. Savasta

Fig. 12 Antonio Savasta
(AP/Wide World Photos)

agreed with that. He said that they were not interested in military information, but that they wanted to show the Italian people that I was a war

Fig. 13 Ransacked study

criminal. I decided I would give very short answers if at all possible. That
generally worked.

The trial sessions were laborious in that I did not speak Italian very
well. We spent a lot of time using an Italian-English dictionary. It turned
out that they used the questions and answers in their communiqués,
which were periodically distributed to the public. As it turned out, however, they were also used by the police.

While ransacking our Verona apartment (Figure 13), they took a lot
of my personal files. Although we kept nothing classified in the apartment, they found enough material that interested them. For instance,
they found a list of my awards and decorations for combat in Vietnam.
They used the award narratives as prima facie evidence of me being a war
criminal. That caused me to rue the day that in the military, award narrative actions were usually inflated. They also found the telephone tree used
by the LANDSOUTH wives' club, which listed the telephone numbers
of the ladies, in accordance with their husband's position in the headquarters. Thus, they had an organizational chart of a NATO headquarters.

Some of the questions gave me an insight into their political thinking,
such as:

Savasta: "Tell us the overall plan that you Americans have for the control of Italy, politically, economically and militarily."

Dozier: "There is no such plan; and even if there was one of that significance, I would not be privy to it, since I served at a very low level, not involving strategy."

Savasta: "I don't believe you. You Americans have done this before in Europe."

Dozier: "I do not know what you are talking about. When and how did we do that? Please give me details."

Savasta: "After WWII, Americans initiated the Marshall Plan, which subjugated Western Europe politically, economically and militarily."

Dozier: "The Marshall Plan was designed to rebuild, not subjugate, Western Europe in the wake of WWII. In contrast, the Soviet Union did in fact subjugate Eastern Europe after the war. How do you explain that?"

Savasta changed the subject.

We spent quite a lot of time on the organization of a NATO headquarters. This was the result of them finding the ladies' telephone tree. We also talked about the purpose and mission of NATO. They seemed convinced that NATO was an American organization that posed a threat to European communism and the Soviet Union, rather than as a defensive organization against the Warsaw Pact.

Fig. 14 Cesare Di Lenardo (ANSA)

I never convinced them otherwise.

One of the guards, Di Lenardo, tried to brainwash me.

One day during the second or third week into the kidnapping, Cesare Di Lenardo, who seemed to be the most politically oriented of the bunch (Figure 14 in police custody), gave me a 12-page treatise, in Italian, on the philosophy of the Red Brigades. I skimmed it and put it away under the bunk. A couple of days later he came in, questioned me on it, and wanted to discuss it. I flunked and had to admit that I had not read it in detail. He was disappointed and somewhat offended. So, for about a week, he and I would sit on the bunk and translate the thing using an Italian-English dictionary.

The treatise was filled with rhetoric that made very little sense to me. We would come to a passage full of somewhat senseless language and I would ask him if he really believed what we were reading. He would try to explain, but he could tell that I wasn't buying into it, which really disappointed him. After we finished translating the treatise and it still was obvious that I wasn't buying into its philosophy, he voiced his frustration by saying, "If we can't convert you, maybe we can at least make you neutral."

It became apparent during the inquisition that quite a few of the questions were generated by the material they took from our Verona apartment. In addition to talking about political and military issues, associated with portraying me as a war criminal, they became interested in the personalities of officers at LANDSOUTH, most of whom I knew very few details about. For instance:

> Savasta: "How well do you know the family of General Santini, the former CINC of LANDSOUTH?"

> Dozier: "I knew General Santini in an official capacity. I have met his wife, a very nice lady, but I know nothing about his family."

What would appear in a resulting communiqué would be a complete rundown on General Santini's wife: where they lived, her telephone number, etc.

When such a communiqué was found by the authorities, they would check with my wife, who would tell them that I had no idea about that level of detail regarding General Santini's wife. However, it did lead the authorities to believe that I was still alive. It became obvious that they were getting the information from the wives' club telephone tree.

About a week into the kidnapping, Di Lenardo and Savasta came into the tent with a sign in Italian that espoused Red Brigades propaganda. They wanted me to hold it in front of myself while they took a photo. I told them I would not do that. They replied that they would pin it to my shirt if necessary, but that they were going to take a photo anyway.

I then thought that this might be an opportunity

Fig. 15 Propaganda photo

to get a signal out to my wife. So, I agreed to hold the sign with my fingers in a 'V.' They would not allow that, so I next tried to hold it with my middle fingers pointing out. That upset them, so they very carefully placed my fingers on the edge of the sign and took the photo (Figure 15). They published the photo in one of their communiqués, which was shown to my wife. After all of the trouble with placing my fingers on the sign, the photo clearly showed my left hand and USMA ring (not shown in this photo). My wife noticed this right away. It was the first real indication that I was alive.

There is more to this photo session that is rather humorous. They came back the next day and said that the photos did not turn out, so that they needed to take some more. They placed my fingers as they had before, took the photos and left. This happened twice more. Before the final session, I asked Di Lenardo, "How many more times do you need to do this?" He called me a smart ass.

Toward the end of the kidnapping, they took some more photos. When I again asked how many times would this session take before they got it right, he again told me to shut up and again called me a smart ass. By the way, it took four times.

The photos had multiple purposes for the Red Brigades, but for my wife and the authorities, they showed that I was still alive, as indicated by the beard growth.

Just before I was rescued, Savasta, in one of his "Peoples' Court" sessions, began asking me questions regarding U.S. nuclear storage facilities in the AFSOUTH region. I reminded him that we had agreed not to discuss anything TOP SECRET. He replied that they knew all about them and that he wanted to know if his information was correct. I refused to talk about the subject and he left. That evening, dinner was late. I thought "here it comes." They were going to get rough with what had heretofore been rather benign treatment. It turns out that wasn't the case at all; they were simply having trouble in the kitchen. Dinner came about three hours late with an apology.

Quite frankly, I knew virtually nothing about the storage sites, only that they existed, so I would not have had to fake a lack of knowledge if I had been pushed. It turns out that an Army War College classmate was the commander of the sites. Several times he invited me to visit some of them and meet his soldiers. Each time I told him that I was in a NATO position and had no business intruding into a strictly American affair. The "Need to Know Policy" that is prevalent in the U.S. intelligence community stood me in good stead in this case.

I wondered why they became interested in the nuclear storage sites in the first place. It wasn't until I was being debriefed after my rescue that I learned that when Savasta asked about them, an Italian magazine had written a detailed account of the sites. It was so detailed that it concerned the Allied intelligence community. When I returned to the U.S. after my rescue, Senator Howard Baker, head of the Senate Intelligence

Committee, called me to his office to personally debrief me regarding questions I was asked.

My Wife's Experience

Judy was a very strong woman. By this time, we had been married for 25 years. She had experienced all of the trials and tribulations connected with being a military spouse: family separations; having children in foreign countries; traveling overseas with a baby while pregnant with another; living in sub-standard housing and learning how to live in various countries; as well as meeting new friends every few years. Our assignment to Verona was par for the course. It was a stop on the way to an anticipated assignment to a U.S. unit in Germany.

Fig. 16 Dozier kitchen area

In addition to my military duties, as previously mentioned, I was also the community leader of our small American community, which included an American school, the auditorium of which was used on Sundays for chapel services. Judy rapidly became involved with the school and other American community activities. We actively socialized with other allied officers that I worked with in the headquarters, to include playing duplicate bridge with retired Italian officers. We also became good friends with some of the Italians living in our apartment building.

Even though many of these details have previously been discussed, on the evening of the kidnapping, we were having a quick drink in the kitchen before having a light dinner. Our intention was to go to a community council meeting with our small American community. When the doorbell on our floor rang without the building bell ringing first, Judy expressed concern. I told her not to worry, it could be one of our neighbors. She then went back to preparing dinner. After I let the two "plumbers" in, she stepped out of the kitchen to see what was going on (Figure 16). She saw me talking to two young men dressed in blue coveralls, and sporting black moustaches and beards with each carrying a tool bag. It later turned out that the moustaches and beards were stage makeup. When I explained to her that they wanted to check our apartment for leaks, she returned to the kitchen.

While we were in the washroom/utility room checking for leaks, Judy remembered that she had used the washing machine that day, so she came around to the washroom. I was on my hands and knees looking under sinks and toilets searching for leaks when she leaned over the shoulders of the two "plumbers" to tell me about the washing machine. This took the two young men by surprise. We later learned that they had planned to take me down in the constricted area of the washroom/utility room. We also later learned that they had made a very detailed reconnaissance of our apartment.

On that night, the two men started to ask me questions in Italian regarding where else we might look. As I didn't understand some of the words, I told them we needed to go back to the kitchen where I keep an Italian-English dictionary. We then all went back to the kitchen. Judy continued fixing dinner while I was looking up the words in the dictionary.

The two "plumbers" were standing side-by-side blocking the kitchen door (back to Figure 16). As she looked up at them, they began to pull objects out of their tool bags that she at first didn't recognize. It soon became apparent that the objects were silenced pistols. Judy immediately dropped to her knees as the larger of the two jumped on my back. The smaller of the two, Savasta, grabbed Judy, still on her knees and put a pistol to her head and told her, "Shut up or we'll kill your husband." That was the only English spoken. She shouted, "Honey, do as they say." Since I was having a fight, I didn't hear her, which led to the look she gave me when I later told her the same thing.

After we were both immobilized, a calmness came over Judy. She decided not to scream, thinking that she might get one scream out, but that would get me hurt and she also would possibly get injured. She then began to get clues as to what was going on. The two men told her several times that they were members of the Red Brigades. She thought that they wanted her to be able to tell the authorities who was behind this incident, in case others took credit for it. She also noticed that while I was lying on my back in the hallway, they would check my breathing and pulse. That implied to her that they didn't want us dead right then.

Judy also discovered that the chains used to immobilize her had little locks to hold them together. And, much to her surprise, each lock had a key. This gave her another clue regarding what they intended to do to her. After she was immobilized, they dragged her into a corner of the kitchen to get her out of the way.

When they brought the trunk in to take me away, she got a good look at it and was later able to describe it to the authorities.

Once I was taken away, they blindfolded her and, with the chains in place, dragged her down the hall into the washroom. While being dragged, the blindfold slipped down over her nose, which made breathing difficult. She complained about it and a hand reached down and adjusted the blindfold, another clue. They left Judy in the washroom, turned out the lights and locked the door. She knew that some of them were still in the apartment because she could hear them using the call buttons for the maid. They also turned the lights on and off while ransacking the apartment. The apartment had a separate area for a live-in maid, in which the buzzers associated with the various rooms were located. The washroom was in the maid's area. We had no maid, by the way.

She started to experiment with the locks and keys, but since it was obvious the kidnappers were still in the apartment, she decided to wait. Sure enough, they came back to check on her. This happened several times. The last time they did something a little different. They brought in our portable radio, tuned it to an all-music station, put a pillow under her head and unzipped her skirt. Judy thought the worst about the unzipped skirt, but they just moved it back and forth to make sure it wasn't too tight and left.

She figured that they were now gone for good. She tried one of the keys in one of the locks, but it didn't work. It turns out that they left the wrong key in that lock. Judy had better results with the next lock. When she unlocked it, it released the chain that ran between the ankle and wrist chains. This gave her mobility. She then rubbed her head on the pillow until the blindfold no longer covered

Fig. 17
Hot water heater

her eyes. As a result, she was able to
see the pilot light in our hot water
heater (Figure 17). She now knew
what room of the house she was
in. Although her wrists and ankles
were still chained, she was able to
move around and raise her legs so
that she could reach the washroom
light switch and turn a light on
with her foot.

Judy decided to make an effort
to attract the attention of the downstairs neighbors. Early evening
is quiet time in an Italian apartment, so she decided to make as
much noise as possible. She leaned
against the washing machine and

Fig. 18 Judy Dozier leaving the
apartment (AP/Wide World Photos)

began banging on it with her shoulders and knees. She put the banging
in a rhythm, three bangs and a call for help in Italian, hoping that those
below wouldn't think that the noisy Americans upstairs were working
on something in the apartment. The daughter of the family below heard
her, but sure enough, she thought the folks upstairs were working in the
apartment.

The daughter then went to another room in her apartment to watch a
television special. After the special was over, she went back to her bathroom and found that the noise was still going on and was in a rhythm.
She told her parents, who figured something was wrong. Her parents
then went across the hall to tell a couple, with whom we were good
friends, about the noise. After listening closely to the noise, this friend,
Aldo Marulli, tried the front door, but got no answer. He then went onto
a balcony around our penthouse and broke a bathroom window. After
he entered the apartment, Judy was not hard to find. She was in the
only lighted room in the apartment. The Marullis called the police, who,
when they arrived, cut the remaining chains, thus freeing Judy and then
alerting the world about the kidnapping (Figure 18).

From that point on, Judy was headline news for quite some time. For safety, the NATO headquarters decided that she should move to an apartment in the NATO compound, which she did. Our daughter, Cheryl, then a 2nd lieutenant in the USAF, stationed at Rhein Main AFB in Germany, was flown down to Vicenza, then driven to Verona that night. A couple of days later, our son, Scott, who was going to college in Fort Walton Beach, Florida, was flown to Europe under a fake name so that he could join the family.

The kidnapping interrupted a planned Dozier family holiday at Berchesgarten, Germany, a military R & R resort. We also had invited my sister and her daughter to join us. Judy decided that my sister and her daughter should come over anyway. Thus, after a couple of days in the NATO HQ apartment, she insisted that she be allowed to return to our apartment, where there would be room for everyone.

Judy's ride back to our apartment in a NATO staff car was chaotic. The press had not had any access to Judy up until this time. Press vehicles pursued the staff car and periodically raced ahead in order to block its progress so as to get photos. After finally getting back to the apartment, she found that the paparazzi were waiting. They pushed their way into the building when the front door was opened, with some even crowded into the elevator when she went upstairs. All of this activity annoyed our neighbors. Judy decided that this was an intolerable problem that should be immediately solved.

U.S. officers in the headquarters worked out a solution with the media. The solution was:

- Judy would not give any exclusive interviews; interviews would be pooled.

- To eliminate the dangerous vehicle chases, a daily schedule of her activities would be provided.

Fig. 19 Balcony photo op (AP/Wide World Photos)

- Judy would appear on the balcony of our apartment at a certain time each day, in order for the media to get their photo ops (Figure 19).
- The media would stay down on the street and would not enter the building.

Judy closely cooperated with the authorities after her release. Scott had joined Judy in Verona during her debriefing by the Italian police. The police brought in a sketch artist to assist with identifying the kidnappers. However, a communications problem soon developed in that Judy's Italian was as poor as the sketch artist's English. Judy suggested that Scott, who was an accomplished artist, assist the Italian sketch artist. This worked well. From Judy's descriptions, Scott drew sketches of the alleged kidnappers. Judy also was able to describe the trunk used to carry me off.

From the sketches, Judy later went through police mug books and was able to identify the terrorists who had come to the door or who had entered the apartment. She realized that the Red Brigades had made a thorough reconnaissance of the apartment, posing as sales people, pollsters and utility workers. For instance, when asked who had entered the apartment, she mentioned meter readers (plural). It turns out that one individual had the meter reading responsibility for the building. The three who had come to read the water, gas and electricity meters were probably all members of the Red Brigades, as were some of those who came to the door selling various items.

Fig. 20 MG Walt Ulmer

After about four weeks, Judy felt that she could no longer help the authorities. In addition, Cheryl needed to get back to work at Rhein Main. My sister and her daughter, plus Scott, had already gone back to the U.S. Friends in the Frankfurt, Germany area had previously invited Judy to stay with them, so she and Cheryl traveled to Frankfurt by train. Our friends stationed in Germany provided the moral support she needed during the rest of the kidnapping period.

In Germany, Judy stayed in the home of a good friend with whom she had grown up in Washington, and who had married one of my classmates. They and other friends would get together each day for coffee and to chat. One of her other friends was Marty Ulmer, whose husband, MG Walt Ulmer (Figure 20), was the CG of the 3rd Armored Division, stationed nearby. Walt would routinely keep the ladies informed on the latest events regarding my kidnapping

Judy related that on the morning of my rescue, she awoke to a beautiful German winter day. It gave her an uplifting feeling. Little did she know that the previous day Walt had received intelligence that I had been killed. Since false rumors to that effect had circulated before, Walt decided in this case not to mention it until he could confirm the report. So, on the morning I was rescued, Walt received the news and immediately called the home where Judy was staying. When Judy was told who was calling, she picked up the phone and asked Walt, "Should I be standing up or sitting down for this morning's news?" Walt replied that "It doesn't make any difference; Jim has been rescued."

Red Brigades Reconnaissance

The Red Brigades reconnaissance prior to the kidnapping was extensive and thorough. It began with a group sitting at a sidewalk café (Figure 21) across the street from the NATO headquarters (Figure 22). My photo had been in the local papers, so they knew who they were looking for. They watched officers come and go. The first one they followed was a USMC lieutenant colonel who fit my general description. But pretty soon they figured out that he was not the general. They also followed a U.S. Navy captain. The terrorists figured that with all the stripes on his sleeves and the

Fig. 21 Red Brigades sidewalk cafe

Fig. 22 NATO HQ entrance

Fig. 23 Kidnappers' observation point

braid on his hat, he must be very important. Again, they soon figured out that he was not the general.

In their frustration, they went to a toy store not too far from the NATO headquarters that specialized in toy soldiers, a very popular hobby in Italy. There, they found a booklet that depicted the uniforms of the various NATO nations. They picked out an American general's green uniform and identified me. It sounds a little weird, but as I mentioned previously, the members of the Red Brigades had very little understanding of NATO and the U.S. role in it. Instead, they tended to feed on their own rhetoric.

Once they identified me, they initiated their pre-kidnapping reconnaissance. They began to follow me while I was transported in a NATO sedan between our apartment and the headquarters. As previously mentioned, my regular driver was a member of the Carabinieri, the Italian paramilitary law enforcement agency. DiNardo was well schooled in defensive driving techniques, as was I. However, neither of us became aware that we were being followed.

The technique that the Red Brigades used was to follow us on a motor scooter or a motorbike for a couple of blocks, then hand us off to another team using walkie-talkie radios. This way they hoped to avoid being obvious. Since we traveled in a sea of motorbikes and scooters anyway, neither DiNardo nor I noticed that we were being followed. Every day, we tried to vary our routes, but each route had the same "choke point" at either the beginning or end. Using this technique, the terrorists were able to

Fig. 24 Kidnappers' door view

determine the different routes that we used to go back and forth to the headquarters.

Once they were familiar with the different routes we traveled, they moved into the immediate area of the apartment and set up an observation point in a hospital parking lot across the river from our apartment (Figure 23). The parking lot and adjacent riverbank were a sort of a lovers' lane, in that young couples would use the location for a moment for themselves. Judy would, from time to time, mention that different couples were in the parking lot, as she used the nearby street to go back and forth to the dry cleaners.

From the parking lot vantage point, Red Brigades members were able to pin down the routine of the people in the apartment building, as well as that of the surrounding neighborhood. Once they were familiar with the different routines, they moved into the immediate area of the apartment itself (Figure 24). They often mingled with the bus stop crowds, and even went through the Dempster Dumpsters, building intelligence on us.

American trash was easy to identify. We were still using brown paper commissary bags, while the Italians had already moved on to plastic. They also discovered that even though there was a doorbell system that controlled access to the building, there also was a commercial sports office on the ground floor. The counter girl who worked there would automatically open the front building door when her bell was rung, without asking for identification. Of course, that was the way they were able to enter the building posing as pollsters, sales people and kidnappers. All in all, the reconnaissance took about six weeks. It was professional and very thorough.

Rescue by the NOCS

After exactly six weeks in captivity, I was rescued on the morning of January 28, 1982, by an Italian National Police SWAT team called the NUCLEO OPERATIVO CENTRALE di SICUREZZA (NOCS), assisted by a U.S. special operations unit. However, during the previous six weeks, an enormous effort to find me was put forth by both Italian and U.S. authorities.

On the night that I was kidnapped, the U.S. ambassador to Italy, Maxwell Raab, was in northern Italy on embassy business. As soon as he learned of the kidnapping, he immediately drove back to Rome during a blizzard. He went straight to the Italian minister of interior to get the latest information available. Ambassador Raab was a forceful individual, a New York lawyer, who had previously been involved with spy exchanges with the Warsaw Pact. He strongly insisted that the ministry pull out all the stops in their efforts to locate and rescue me. He also told the Italian authorities that he would make available to them U.S. resources as necessary. The Italian government responded with a massive investigation, led by Umberto Improta, a senior Italian police officer, and a massive manhunt, involving every law enforcement organization in the country. I was told that more than 6,000 members of Italian law enforcement and military organizations were searching for me.

Ambassador Raab then personally coordinated the U.S. support effort, which involved U.S. intelligence, law enforcement agencies and special operations units. He quickly resolved jurisdictional disputes that developed in the U.S. special operations commands between USEUCOM and JSOC. He insisted that there be a well-coordinated effort on the part of the Italians. He was largely successful, even though some parochialism still prevailed. For instance, after I was rescued, a Carabinieri general apologized for not rescuing me first.

The manhunt in northern Italy was so intense that even drug trafficking came to a halt. Nevertheless, about four weeks into the investigation, the authorities had run out of leads, so they decided to go back through the prisons and re-interrogate those already arrested. These efforts paid off. One of the persons interrogated was a fairly big drug dealer who had connections to the Red Brigades. He told the authorities where to find the driver who had driven me from Verona to Padova. That was the break that they needed.

Fig. 25 Volinia, the driver (ANSA)

They found Volinia, the driver, in bed with his girlfriend and arrested them both (Figure 25). They were interrogated within earshot of each other and both broke down. Volinia showed the authorities where he had picked up the trunk and where he took it. From that point on, there was a coordinated effort between the Italian authorities and the U.S. Embassy, assisted by a U.S. special operations unit to determine if I was still at that location. Once it was established that I was still at the same place, the NOCS executed a rescue plan.

A 10-man team under the command of Edoardo Perna hurriedly left Rome for Padova. They decided that a daytime rescue was the best course of action.

Working with local authorities, the team formed a security cordon around the apartment building. One element of the team prepared to break in the front door of the apartment. The team had been informed that the kidnappers, sitting in their boredom, (Figure 26) quite frequently watched the parking lot in front of the downstairs supermarket. The team coordinated with local authorities to create a diversion in the parking lot so that the kidnappers were distracted. Once this was done, the rescue element broke in the front door of the apartment.

Indeed, the diversion worked. What a kidnapper saw that morning was a truck unloading a backhoe and an air compressor for a jackhammer into the parking lot. Soon, workers began digging up the parking lot. At one point, a commercial van pulled up in front of the supermarket. Out of the van came two individuals dressed in tight fitting clothes, ski masks and carrying automatic weapons. One of the kidnappers later testified that he thought they were members of the Red Brigades,

Fig. 26 Supermarket parking lot

robbing the supermarket in order to finance operations. The Red Brigades routinely did that from time to time. However, as more security showed up, it was evident to them that a rescue attempt was underway, but by this time the NOCS had broken through the front door.

They broke through using one of the NOCS, a former wrestler, nicknamed "The Elephant," as a battering ram. They loaded him up with two 40-pound protective vests and gave him a running start. When he hit the door, he took the entire frame down with him. Later, he complained that all of those following stepped on him before he could get up. One of the NOCS told me that it took about six seconds for them to find me and neutralize those inside.

In the event of a rescue attempt, the kidnappers previously had decided not to resist. They took advantage of an Italian law, called the Penitence Law, which stated that if a convicted member of a terrorist organization cooperated with the authorities, whatever sentence had been adjudged would be cut in half. Not a shot was fired, and with one exception, no one was badly hurt.

On the morning of the rescue, the first indication I had that something unusual was going on was when the walls of the tent billowed. This occurred while I was sitting on the bunk reading *1984* for the second time. The billowing meant that someone had opened the door of the room, which created air currents. I looked out under the inner flap of the tent to see who might be coming in. What I saw was a hand reach through the outer flap of the tent to hand the guard, Ciucci, sitting in his chair (Figure 27), a silenced pistol (Figure 28). This was unusual because the guards were never armed. Within a split second, another figure burst through the flap of the tent and knocked Ciucci down. Ciucci got up and was knocked down again. Then another man, wearing tight fitting clothes and a ski mask, pushed his way into my portion of the tent.

Fig. 27 Kidnapper's chair

Fig. 28 Silenced pistol (Courtesy Polizia Di Stato)

Fig. 29 Weapons cache

I wasn't sure what was going on. My first thoughts were that I was witnessing a dispute between rival elements of the Red Brigades. Such a dispute previously had led to the death of Aldo Moro, a prominent Italian politician and prime minister, who was killed by this same group several years earlier. The second person kept telling me he was a policeman, but even though still connected to the cot, I tried to push him away.

Fig. 30 Ransacked apartment

I wasn't buying what he was saying. He quickly pulled off his ski mask so I could see his face. That convinced me he was who he said he was, so I stopped reacting.

This NOCS member then said that they needed to get me out of the building quickly, since they believed it might be rigged for demolition. Although the apartment was a veritable arsenal (Figure 29), containing lots of guns, ammunition and explosives, fortunately no charges were set. As I was being hustled out of the apartment, I noticed that every drawer was pulled out and every cupboard was open and that all contained some form of arms, ammunition or explosives (Figure 30). I also noticed that four of the kidnappers were spread-eagled on the floor of the entrance way. When one of the females began to cry, one of the NOCS placed his foot on her head and told her to be quiet.

Then began for me, and I'm not being flippant when I write this, the most exciting time of the whole experience: a wild, noontime rush-hour ride through downtown Padova in an Italian police car! It goes without saying that the streets of this old European city were crowded and narrow. I believe that in general, Italians are very good drivers. Maybe Naples is an exception! However, I also believe that the drivers one sees are the survivors. Their idea of driving an automobile is to keep the engine turning at 4,000 to 5,000 rpms, while controlling the motion of the vehicle with the clutch, brake and liberal use of the horn.

I was thrown into the back seat of the lead police car of several, in which a police officer got in on either side of me, and off we went. Lights were flashing, horns were blaring, and all of the vehicles were using their sirens. People and vehicles parted like the Red Sea as we made our way uptown. The streets were not nearly as wide as shown on the map (Figure 31), and they certainly weren't as straight. We went on and off the sidewalks. I looked at the speedometer just one time and we were doing 140 kph (about 87 mph). We entered one intersection as a police car entered from the cross street. We both spun out. I thought to myself, "After six weeks, it all boils down to a traffic accident," but we finally made it to the city hall in one piece.

Fig. 31 Map to city hall

It was cold that morning and that was just about all the excitement that I needed. The very smell of freedom was invigorating. We made our way upstairs to the chief's office. Prior to the photo being taken, I rather naively asked if he could get my headquarters on the line so I could report back in. He turned to his secretary, but she was gone. Someone had sent her for coffee!

The poor chief was unfamiliar with the long distance telephone system

Fig. 32 With the chief and the phone

interconnections with the NATO bases in that part of Italy. When I asked him personally to do something that he was not able to do, he was greatly embarrassed. What you see in the photo above (Figure 32) was the result of about a 10-minute goat rope period. He kept at it until he was able to get my headquarters on the phone so that I was able to report back in.

Figure 33 shows the cup of coffee that caused all the problems with the telephone. Since I am a coffee lover and had been without coffee for six weeks, one can just imagine how good that coffee tasted. The picture also shows the warm-up suit that the Red Brigades provided. A little anecdote goes along with the clothes. In addition to all the things the authorities found in that Padova apartment was a ledger that contained an expense account that the guards had been maintaining. One of the line items in the account was an item that listed the Italian equivalent of $50 for a "uniform for the prisoner." I still have that warm-up suit. There was a price tag in the collar that listed the real price at about $14. If there is

Fig. 33 Phone to HQ and coffee

a moral associated with this story, it is that in almost all terror organizations, there exists a hard core. But also, in nearly all of them, there are fringe elements, who at times are nothing more than common criminals. In this case, at least one of the guards couldn't resist making a lira or two off of what they had been doing. They had been ripping off their higher HQ!

Little did I realize at the time as to how fast the news of my rescue had traveled. I was soon joined at the city hall by General McFadden, CG of SETAF (Southern European Task Force) headquartered at Vicenza. McFadden was an intelligence officer and during the ride back to Vicenza, our conversation revolved around what kind of information the Red Brigades had been able to glean from me. I assured him that I had abided by the rules as outlined in the Code of Conduct. I suggested that to fully answer the question, I should be debriefed at Vicenza by U.S. intelligence as soon as possible. General McFadden set that up and the debriefings started that night and lasted for several days. However, I was never thoroughly debriefed by the Italian authorities.

Fig. 34 Hamburger

At Vicenza, I was taken to the base dispensary, where I was given a quick medical checkup. When the doctors were satisfied that I was in reasonable shape, I asked to shave and shower. I was taken to the barber shop, where six weeks of beard and moustache were removed. While in the barber shop half shaved, I received a telephone call from President Reagan. He asked how I was doing and was I being properly taken care of. I assured him that I was in pretty good shape, all things considered. He then asked me if it might be possible for me to join him at the National Prayer Breakfast in Washington the next week. Again, being naïve, I told him that I had been out of the loop for six weeks and that I had a lot of catching up to do regarding my job. He said that he understood and we chatted for a few more minutes. Within 30 minutes, I received a call from the chief of staff of the Army's office telling me that they were arranging for me to return to the U.S. that weekend for the Prayer Breakfast. Lesson learned. Then I was asked if I was hungry. I said I was and I was brought a hamburger (Figure 34) for a late lunch.

Judy was flown down from Frankfurt that afternoon in an Army aircraft. We spent the next two nights at the guest quarters in Vicenza just catching up. Before leaving for Verona, I participated in the first of many press conferences (Figure 35).

Security was very tight while we made preparations for our trip back

Fig. 35 Press conference

to the U.S. We decided that U.S. Major Mario Gargiulo, aide to CINC LANDSOUTH (Figure 36, third on the right), would accompany us. Mario spoke fluent Italian and was very adept at doing the pick and shovel work associated with travel. We flew from Vicenza up to Rhein Main in an

Fig. 36 Dr. Guido Papalia, Jim and Major Mario Gargiulo

Army aircraft, then boarded a USAF C-141 medevac flight headed to Andrews AFB, Maryland, just outside of Washington, D.C.

Several hours before landing at Andrews, the pilot asked me to come to the cockpit. They had a radio call from the Pentagon that they wanted me to answer. I put on a headset, and to my surprise, I began talking to Colonel Mike Vargosko, a former protégé of mine at Fort Hood. He was in the Office of Army Public Affairs in the Pentagon and wanted to give me a heads-up regarding the reception I could expect when we landed at Andrews. He could not go into details over the radio, but wanted me to know that there would be plenty of VIPs. He further told me that he would be managing my personal appearances at various functions. Little did I realize at that point what I was in for. However, I knew that with Mike running interference, I was in good hands.

There was a near incident during our landing at Andrews. The instrument landing system (ILS) on the plane malfunctioned. Visibility was bad and when we broke out of the 500-foot ceiling, we were lined up between the two runways. The pilot was forced to go around and try again. The wingspan on the C-141 was about 150 feet wide and the pilot had to make his turns below the ceiling in order to keep the runway in sight. Of course, we didn't know all of this until we landed. A pilot friend in the reception group told me that they held their breaths while the pilot was going around. My friend said that the pilot performed a first-class piece of airmanship.

United States Tour

When we finally landed at Andrews and debarked the aircraft, we were greeted by a huge reception party. What a reception party it was! The sizeable crowd included:

Fig. 37 VP George H. W. Bush

- The vice president of the United States, George H. W. Bush (Figure 37) and his wife, Barbara.

- The U.S. Army chief of staff, General Shy Meyer and his wife.

- Judy's closest friend, Lois Hanmer, and her husband, Read.

- Two of our closest friends, Colonel Bob Molinelli and his wife, Donna.

- My old friend Colonel Mike Vargosko, who would be handling our itinerary.

- Several senators and congressmen.

- A host of other dignitaries.

After exchanging greetings on the tarmac, VP Bush said that he was on a pretty tight schedule, but he wanted us to ride with him to Fort Myer, Virginia, where we would be staying. It was a delightful ride. The Bushes were very friendly people and easy to be with. We talked a little about my experience and how it was handled from the Washington end. VP Bush dropped us off at the Fort Myer guest quarters, Washington Hall, telling us that he looked forward to seeing us at the National Prayer Breakfast, coming up in a day or two.

Mike Vargosko took over from there. He led us on a whirlwind tour of morning television news shows, a press conference in the Pentagon

briefing room, a meeting with the secretary of defense, Caspar Weinberger, a visit
to the State Department, and a visit to the
NSA, where we met one of the NSA persons who was instrumental in finding me.
I profusely thanked her.

Since Judy's parents lived in Washington, we were soon reunited with them, as
well as with friends in the Washington
area. However, since we were under pretty
tight security, friends came to see us at
Washington Hall, rather than us going to
meet them. We enjoyed the reunion with
all our friends, as we did with each other.
As much as we wanted to spend time
alone (Figure 38), Mike's program kept us
hopping from one venue to another.

Fig. 38 Together again

On the morning of the National Prayer Breakfast, we were picked
up by an Army sedan and taken to the White House. We waited in the
Diplomatic Reception Room until President and Mrs. Reagan came
downstairs. We exchanged greetings and shortly thereafter entered his
limousine to travel to the Prayer Breakfast. Like the Bushes, the Reagans
also were very gracious and easy to talk with. President Reagan knew
that I had been awarded the Purple Heart in Vietnam. That started a
conversation about him getting shot. At one point he said that when he
was shot, "It hurt like hell!"

At the Prayer Breakfast, we sat at the head table, along with various
dignitaries. After the breakfast was over, we went back to the White house
in the limousine. The Prayer Breakfast was held in the same hotel where
the president had been shot. As we left the parking garage, he pointed
out the area on the sidewalk where the shooting took place. Mrs. Reagan
was silent. We went back to the White House and into the Oval Office.
Mrs. Reagan and Judy excused themselves to tour the White House, and
the president and I sat in front of the fireplace (Figure 39) chatting.

One subject I brought up was when the kidnappers ransacked our
apartment in Verona, they took a folder that contained all of my 1981

Fig. 39 Jim with President Reagan

income tax backup records. Most folks, when they are assigned overseas, do their best to be good citizens by voting and paying their income taxes on time. I was no exception. When I found out that I had no records with which to file my income tax, I had a problem. It was now February and the April 15 income tax filing deadline was fast approaching. I knew that I was going to meet the president, so I thought that would be an opportunity to go right to the top with my income tax problem. So, while we were sitting in front of the fireplace, I told him the whole story. He just looked at me, smiled, and said, "Good luck." I filed for an extension and paid my taxes a little late.

Soon, an aide came in to tell the president that President Mubarak of Egypt had just arrived. President Reagan said "I had better not keep him waiting." I again thanked the president and excused myself. On the way out, I met President Mubarak in the outside hallway and shook his hand. It was quite a day.

The next day, along with a security detail, we flew by commercial air to Fort Walton Beach, Florida, the first stop on a five-stop odyssey. Our son, Scott, had returned to college at Fort Walton Beach and was working part time in a bar called the Green Knight, a real Bubba bar. The band was named Poor White Trash. We were billeted in the VIP quarters at nearby Eglin AFB.

The security detail had sent an advance team in the morning to check out the Green Knight. When they returned, they were somewhat concerned about how to dress and still hide their weapons, since most of the daytime patrons were dressed in T-shirts and jeans. It turned out that they really didn't need to worry. They fit right in, since some of the evening patrons had carry permits and were openly displaying their weapons. We had a great evening. In the interest of peace and good will, they did, however, let the Black member of the security team have the night off. It was Florida at night in a Bubba bar.

A day or so later, we flew to Tallahassee, Florida, on a Florida Army National Guard aircraft, for lunch with Governor Bob Graham and his staff. The governor was very cordial, as was his staff. Also included at the lunch were the state representative from my district and his staff, the district which included my hometown, Arcadia, Florida. It was a very nice visit.

After lunch, we flew by the same aircraft to MacDill AFB, Tampa, Florida. There, we were greeted by the base commander and some old friends, including Colonel Dick Doty and his wife, Gail. Dick, at that time, was the G3 Operations for the Rapid Deployment Joint Task Force, the precursor to the U.S. Central Command, which was headquartered at MacDill. That evening we went to dinner at their home in nearby Brandon. The security detail already had thoroughly checked out the Doty home, which created quite a stir in the neighborhood.

The next day, Dick and I went bass fishing on lakes in nearby Winter Haven. This caused a small problem for the security detail, who had to rent bass boats faster than ours so that they could secure the fishing areas and follow us around while we fished. I don't remember the results of our fishing, but sharing some quiet time with an old friend made it worthwhile. Judy, on the other hand, was able to spend a quiet day with Gail.

The next morning, we flew by USAF helicopter to participate in a welcome home celebration in my hometown, Arcadia, southeast of Tampa. It was a foggy morning, but we took off anyway and headed to Arcadia. When we were in the vicinity of Arcadia, the fog had lifted a bit, but we still had to fly around some more until I spotted a familiar landmark. We finally landed at the Army National Guard armory, where I had first enlisted in 1950.

Arcadia pulled out all the stops for the welcome home ceremony. I learned that children were let out of school and saw them lining the

Fig. 40 Arcadia Welcome Home Parade (Palm Beach Post)

parade route waving flags, while church bells rang. The high school marching band was in full uniform. We rode in a convertible in a parade through downtown (Figure 40).

The parade was followed by speeches from a reviewing stand under a tree called the Tree of Knowledge, which was festooned with yellow ribbons. My high school classmate Joel Mattison was the master of ceremonies. A classmate of my sister, Genie Martin, sang the National Anthem. I made a short speech thanking all who put the event together and remarked that it was good to be home. We had lunch at a downtown restaurant and then went to the home of another of my sister's classmates, Mary Ann Treadwell. There, we had dessert and further caught up on things with old friends.

Later that afternoon, we flew by the same helicopter to Fort Myers, Florida, to participate in the annual Edison Festival of Light evening parade. I was the Grand Marshal. Little did I realize at that time that Fort Myers would be my retirement home. Before the parade began, we had a light dinner at the Royal Palm Yacht Club on the Fort Myers waterfront. We thoroughly enjoyed the warm welcome and the enthusiasm shown by those who watched the parade.

That evening, we flew by helicopter back to MacDill AFB. Thus ending a very long, but sincerely appreciated day.

The next day, we had lunch with a prior acquaintance and fellow Armor officer, General Don Starry, then CINC, Readiness Command. We were also able to visit with a number of old friends who lived in the Tampa area, one of whom was my West Point roommate, Bill Westcott and his wife, Doris.

The following day we flew back to Washington in an aircraft provided by CENTCOM.

Up until this point, we had not had much time to spend with Judy's family (her parents, Bill and Lydia Stimpson, and her brother, Bill, and his wife, Joanne) and our friends (Read and Lois Hanmer, plus several others) who lived in the Washington area. We were able to make up for lost time during the next few days.

Return to Italy

Then, it was time to return to Europe. We flew from Andrews to Dover, Delaware, in a twin-engine U-21 aircraft that had been configured for President Lyndon Johnson to use on his ranch in Texas. Although rather small, it was a very plush aircraft, complete with a bar and telephones.

From Dover, we flew on a C-5, a huge aircraft, to Rhein Main AFB in Germany. We were met by a West Point classmate (MG Jack Woodmansee and his wife, Patty), who took us to a VIP suite in the Rhein Main transit hotel. Later, before we left Rhein Main and returned to Italy, we went with the Woodmansees to a performance of "Tops in Blue," a USAF talent show in which our daughter had a part. She and a partner performed a ballet in concert with "Lady" sung by Kenny Rogers. The next day, we flew by Army aircraft back to Vicenza, Italy.

The Trial of the Kidnappers

Out of consideration for Judy and me, and in order to get us out of the country as soon as possible, the five kidnappers were put on trial immediately after Judy and I returned to Italy.

At that time, terrorist trials in Italy were conducted before a tribunal of three judges. The prosecutor, in this case, was Dr. Guido Papalia (Figure 41). To set the scene, looking from the audience toward the judges, the

Fig. 41 Dr. Papalia,
with Jim and Mario

Fig. 42 Lo Bianco and Balzarani (ANSA)

prisoners were in cages along the wall to the left, with a guard holding a baton standing behind each of them. The three judges were on a dais in the center. The media with their video cameras were along a wall to the right. The prosecutor and defense counsels had desks in front of the judges, with their backs to the audience. The witness chair was to the left, in the space between the judges and counsel's tables. Mario Gargiulo's wife, Norma, also participated in the trial as a translator for Judy and me.

When we were being led into the courtroom, I created a minor incident by walking over to the cages (Figure 42) holding Francesco Lo Bianco and Barbara Balzarani, leaders of the Red Brigades. I had never seen them without their ski masks on, so I wanted to see what they really looked like. This caused Di Lenardo to become very excited and he stood up shouting. The guard behind him used his baton to make him sit down and be quiet. Our escorts quickly made us move on into the courtroom and sit down. Judy and I both testified about our respective experiences.

All 14 people who had been directly involved in the kidnapping were convicted and sentenced to 2–26 years confinement. Under Italian law, a convicted terrorist who cooperates with the authorities could have his/ her sentence reduced, depending on a number of conditions. During our last trip to Italy in the fall of 2018, all had been released except Di Lenardo, who had a bad habit of spitting on guards.

Ending Our Tour in Italy

The issue of whether I remained in Italy to finish my tour or return to an assignment in the U.S. was debated between U.S. and Italian officials. The Italians thought that I was a security risk and wanted me out of the country. The U.S. Army position was not to cut and run, but to show resolve by me finishing my normal tour. In the end, there was a compromise.

Shortly after I returned to Verona, a formal ceremony, complete with honor guard, was held in the courtyard at Palazzo Carli, HQ LAND-SOUTH, during which I formally reported back to duty. I then resumed my normal duties as best I could, considering that I was constantly accompanied by a security detail.

Shortly thereafter, I received an invitation from the White House inviting me to attend a state dinner in honor of President Pertini, then the president of Italy. I asked the chief of staff, AFSOUTH in Naples, if this was a command performance or just a polite request. The answer came back that this was indeed a command performance. Almost immediately, I was contacted by the household goods office in Vicenza to set up a time to pack our household goods for shipment back to the U.S.

After our household goods were packed, we bid our farewells to our friends in Verona, both in and out of the headquarters, and traveled by sedan, first to Rome where we said goodbye to Ambassador Raab and President Pertini, and then to Naples. We spent that evening as houseguests of Admiral Bill Crowe, CINC of AFSOUTH, and his wife. The next morning, we caught a military flight back to Dover, Delaware, where we rented a car to travel to Fort Myer, Virginia. We would stay there in transit quarters for several weeks while waiting for my next assignment.

State Dinner for President Pertini

The state dinner at the White House was quite a grand experience for Judy and me. We were driven to the White House from Fort Myer in an Army sedan. It was pretty much an Italian evening, in honor of President Pertini. When we arrived at the White House, we were ushered again into the Diplomatic Reception Room, where we met Joe Montana, then quarterback of the San Francisco 49ers, and his wife. We had a nice chat during which Joe expressed amazement that he and his wife had been

Fig. 43 President Pertini, Nancy Reagan, President Reagan, Judy and Jim

invited to such an affair. Each of us was assigned a military aide for the evening. The aides briefed us on the specifics of the event. The briefing included the fact that the evening would include notable Italian Americans. After a brief stay in the reception room, we were escorted upstairs to a receiving line, which included President Pertini, plus President and Nancy Reagan (Figure 43).

At dinner, I sat at the same table with President Reagan, President Pertini and Supreme Court Justice Thurgood Marshall. Judy sat at a table with General Alexander Haig and Frank Sinatra. After dinner, we were entertained by songs sung by Frank Sinatra and Perry Como.

All of this was quite an experience for a boy who grew up in Arcadia, Florida.

Intelligence Debriefing

During our stay at Fort Myer awaiting assignment, both Judy and I were thoroughly debriefed by representatives of all of our intelligence agencies and given physicals at Walter Reed Army Hospital. The debriefings were conducted at Fort Meade, Maryland, about 30 miles from Fort Myer. They were organized by a colonel, whom I had known during my service at Fort Hood, Texas. The debriefings were a pooled effort by all of our intelligence agencies. The colonel made a special effort to give each agency direct access to the debriefings, in order to preclude the misunderstandings that sometimes occur when individual agencies debrief separately. In addition, the proceedings were videotaped.

The debriefings lasted for several days. Each morning, Judy and I would be picked up by helicopter at Fort Myer and flown to Fort Meade.

During the debriefings, Judy and I were seated in lounge chairs in a well-lighted room with representatives of the major intelligence agencies (CIA, DIA, FBI, NSA, etc.), who took turns asking questions. In another room, connected via video, were other interested intelligence personnel. When one of the other interested personnel wanted to ask a question, they would send in the question by note and it would be read by the colonel. Thus, everyone who participated heard the same questions and the same answers. It was a well-organized and well-conducted affair.

The results of the debriefings were published in a manual titled "Operation Cannon Trail," which was made available in classified libraries to any others who had a need to know.

One additional book on the kidnapping, to which I contributed, was written by Dr. Richard Oliver Collin, a professor at the University of South Carolina, and Gordon L. Freedman, a television and film producer in Los Angeles. The book is entitled, *Winter of Fire* (Figure 44), the code name the Red Brigades gave to their plan for toppling what they called the corrupt Italian government.

Fig. 44
Winter of Fire

CHAPTER 8

Final Military Tours

After a couple of weeks in Washington, it was time for a further assignment. Normally, general officer assignments are programmed well in advance by the Army hierarchy and administered by the Army General Officer Management Office (GOMO). My unexpected early departure from Italy interrupted that process, so while decisions were being made regarding what to do with me, I was put into a holding pattern and given an office in the Pentagon where I did odd jobs.

During those couple of weeks, Judy and I were able to spend a lot of time with her family and visit old friends in the area.

Assistant Commandant, U.S. Armor School

Shortly, the reassignment wheels finished turning and I was told by GOMO that I would go back to Fort Knox, Kentucky as the assistant commandant (AC) of the Armor School. I was delighted. I would replace BG John Ballantyne, an old friend, who was moving on to another assignment. The commanding general of the Armor School was MG Lou Wagner, whom I had known from my teaching days at West Point. The duties of the AC were to oversee the courses taught by the Armor School and to coordinate the activities of the various troop units on the post that supported the courses of instruction. One of those units, The School Brigade, was commanded by another old friend, Colonel Andy O'Meara, who had been the S-2 (intelligence officer) of the 11th ACR while I was the S-3 (operations officer).

In addition to my formal military duties at Fort Knox, I was very much in demand as a speaker about my kidnapping experience in Italy. Since this would involve travel away from Fort Knox, which would possibly be a conflict with my assigned duties, I asked my friend Colonel Mike Vargosko, who worked in the office of the Chief of Army Public Affairs in the Pentagon, to get the Army to establish a policy regarding such requests. The decision was built around the nature of the request: Would speaking to a given group be beneficial for the Army or the DOD? If so, it had Army approval, but it would have to be coordinated with my duties at Fort Knox. MG Wagner readily agreed to this arrangement.

In 1982, while at Fort Knox, I was the grand marshal of the Kentucky Derby parade and appeared with Willard Scott from NBC, commentary host of the parade. I was also a guest of the governor of Kentucky at his mansion in Lexington. Later, I was asked to drive the pace car for the Daytona 400. NASCAR sent a special airplane for us. I also threw out the first pitch at the opening game of the Louisville Cardinals 1982 season. Unfortunately, I bounced it to the catcher.

The Public Affairs Office (PAO) at Fort Knox was the coordinating agency for such requests. Most from civilian agencies were honored on weekends. Requests from military agencies were honored on a case-by-case schedule. Judy and I would both speak about our kidnapping experiences on these occasions. We called it the "Jim and Judy Show."

One such military request came from the Joint Special Operations University (JSOU). We were to speak at the Dynamics of International Terrorism (DIT) course run by the USAF Special Operations School at Hurlburt Field, Florida. That was the beginning of a 33-year relationship with the DIT course. The DIT course was a weeklong course designed to prepare mid-level leaders for duty in high-risk areas of the world. Judy and I taught a two-hour block on kidnapping avoidance and kidnapping survival. Judy would talk about the family aspects of a kidnapping. I would talk about the details from the victim's standpoint. After Judy died, my daughter, Cheryl, took her place talking about the family aspects. Cheryl, as a serving officer in the USAF, had spent most of the time during the kidnapping in Verona with Judy.

As a firm believer in the power of prayer, I spoke to quite a few church audiences and appeared on the cover of *Guideposts* magazine (Figure 1). While speaking to one such very staid church audience, I mentioned "that when folks are praying for you, you sure as hell know it." As soon as I said it, I knew that I had blundered. There was a silence in the audience that didn't last very long and then the murmuring started. That was not language I should have used in a Southern church.

Fig. 1 Cover of
Guideposts magazine

I went on to explain that during my captivity, I had numerous thoughts of those who I knew were praying for me, to include my very dear friend Sherry Brown and her husband, Charles, who had visited us just prior to the kidnapping. In my mind I could hear her saying over and over again that "I told Jim to be careful and he didn't listen. Now I have to pray that he will come through this okay."

It turns out that is exactly what she told her husband on several occasions.

The Ross Perot Pistols

One morning, my executive officer, Major George O'Kelly, whom I had known at Fort Hood, came into my office all excited. He said that he had just received a call from a colonel in the Pentagon to the effect that Ross Perot wanted to give the rescue team "the best handguns that money could buy." H. Ross Perot, a U.S. Naval Academy graduate and philanthropist, had founded the very successful Electronic Data Systems company and ran a third party presidential campaign in 1992. The colonel asked George if we had any recommendations about handguns. Since neither George nor I were experts on the subject, we suggested that the colonel check with members of the Army staff to obtain their advice.

Several months later, the colonel called to tell us the 9 mm pistols were ready and that the Army was making arrangements for us to

personally deliver them to Italy. MG
George McFadden (Figure 2), who
had been CG of Southern European
Task Force (SETAF) during my tour
in Italy, but was now assigned in the
Washington area, would accompany
me.

I met MG McFadden in Washington and we flew together to John
F. Kennedy Airport in New York City,
where we were to pick up the pistols.
Members of one of our intelligence
services delivered a footlocker full of
the pistols to the airplane. We signed
the receipts and headed off to Rome.
Arrangements had already been made

Fig. 2 MG George McFadden

in Rome for a ceremony, during which we would make speeches and
present them to the rescue team.

When we arrived in Rome, we were greeted by numerous Italian
officials and escorted to a lounge where we awaited the delivery of the
footlocker containing the pistols. Shortly, a very agitated Italian official
entered the room and explained to us that Italian customs had confis-
cated the pistols. Under Italian law, such 9 mm-sized pistols were illegal
for individuals to own and thus we could not present them. All of our
protests were in vain, so after an overnight stay in Rome, we returned to
the United States.

As soon as I returned to Fort Knox, we contacted Ross Perot and I
explained the situation to him. He was disappointed, but unfazed. However, he still wanted to present the pistols to the rescue team. We agreed
that he would re-barrel the pistols so that they would be acceptable under
Italian law. One of our intelligence agencies ultimately delivered the pistols to the rescue team. See one of the pistols with the NOCS coat of
arms (Figure 3).

Life at Fort Knox was enjoyable in spite of the rather fast pace generated by both my military duties, as well as the speaking demands. We
lived in Quarters #5, the large house for many years assigned to the

assistant commandant (AC). George Patton had lived in the house when he was the AC some years before. He enjoyed dogs and devoted most of the basement to them. The basement still smelled like his dogs when we arrived.

Duty at Fort Knox was an enjoyable tour, although fast-paced and much less hectic than duty with NATO, or a tour in the Pentagon. I was able to resume my early morning runs using a 2-mile course around the parade ground and adjacent neighborhood. We also had an opportunity to rejoin old friends with whom we had served during previous assignments.

Fig. 3 Perot Pistol and
NOCS coat of arms

Quarters #5 was a huge house. I had visited there when George Patton was the AC. At that time, he had a cook and maid, which he personally paid for. When we were there, we didn't have either. When we entertained, we did it ourselves for relatively small groups. MG Wagner and his wife did most of the official entertaining, supported by a household staff.

The house itself was multistoried: two main floors, an attic and a basement. We used the attic for storage since the basement continued to smell like the Patton dogs. I also planted a garden in the backyard. One of the other generals on post was a gardener who coached me and also had quite a bit of gardening equipment.

During my relatively short tour at Fort Knox, I had two secretaries. One, Betty, had been there for years and was pretty well set in her ways. She refused to switch to an electric typewriter since she was so close to retirement. She continued to use a manual machine, carbon paper and white-out correction fluid until she left about midway through my tour. She was also hard on my aides.

The second secretary was a lovely young lady who attracted quite a bit of attention from those who stopped by my office. From time to time, many of the junior officers would compliment her on her appearance.

One morning while one young officer was overdoing his compliments, she told him, "Captain, do you know how difficult it is for a woman who has three kids she has to get off to school before she can get to work by 7 a.m., to look routinely gorgeous, day in and day out?" He beat a hasty retreat.

Late during our Fort Knox tour, MG Wagner was replaced by MG Rick Brown, a classmate. As with any new CG, MG Brown wanted to make some changes at Fort Knox in order to leave his stamp on the school. Rick focused on research and development and the upgrading of the academic departments' curricula, leaving the coordination of the troop units to me. Much to the frustration of the academic department heads, Rick would pepper them with suggestions for course changes written on 3-inch square 3M yellow sticky notes. These quickly got the nickname "yellow rain," a term from Vietnam days. It was a little awkward working for a classmate, whom you had known for many years and with whom you had many shared experiences, but we made the best of it.

One such shared experience occurred between General Brown and me. This was along with other classmates who had chosen Armor branch, and who attended the Armor School right after graduation from West Point in 1956. Back then, Judy had gone back to Washington to live with her parents and to finish her degree at George Washington University. I became a "bachelor" and moved into the bachelor officer quarters (BOQ), along with the real bachelors.

In those days, we played a lot of bridge. I teamed up with another bachelor classmate, Jack Woodmansee, to play our married classmates for meals. If we lost, we would take them out to dinner. If they lost, they would invite us to a home-cooked meal. We seldom lost, in that we had developed a signaling protocol known only to Jack and me. We particularly enjoyed playing the Browns, especially when they would become frustrated with each other, which led them to make playing mistakes. On one such tense occasion, Jack held the only remaining trump card. He took it out of his hand, licked the back of it and stuck it on his forehead until it came time to play it. That really frustrated the Browns.

Deputy Commanding General, Fort Hood, Texas

Unbeknownst to me at the time, a further assignment awaited. About a year or so into my Fort Knox tour, GOMO notified me that I had been selected to be an assistant division commander (ADC) of the 7th Mechanized Division at Fort Polk, Louisiana. I flew down to Fort Polk to make arrangements for the transfer and to meet those with whom I would be working. Back home, Judy made preparations for the move. *It was not to be.* Shortly after my trip to Fort Polk, I was selected by an Army promotion board to be a major general, so the orders to Fort Polk were cancelled and replaced by orders to Fort Hood, Texas.

It turned out that LTG Walt Ulmer (Figure 4), who was then CG, III Corps and Fort Hood, and who needed a replacement deputy corps commander (DCC), asked for me as soon as the promotion list was published. LTG Ulmer and I had previously served together in the 2nd Armored Division when MG Patton was the Division CG, Ulmer the ADC and I was a brigade commander. In addition, Judy had spent some time near the Ulmers in Germany during my kidnapping. In fact, as was previously mentioned, it was then MG Ulmer who first informed Judy that I had been rescued.

Serving with and for LTG Ulmer was one of the most symbiotic, enjoyable assignments I had during my time in the military. Walt Ulmer was the epitome of a true leader. He was a 1952 graduate of West Point, an Armor officer, a hero in the Vietnam War and a former commandant of cadets at West Point. In addition, he thoroughly understood leaders and soldiers, to include how the chain of command functioned or didn't function.

Fig. 4 LTG Walt Ulmer, CG III Corps

For instance, we would promulgate a policy, then wait a reasonable period to see how it was being implemented. To check, we would arrange a meeting with enlisted cooks, supply clerks or maintenance personnel. He would ask soldiers what they thought of his new policy on supply or maintenance. Usually they would give him feedback, pro or con, regarding the policy and we would accordingly change it as necessary. However, if the answer came back "what policy?" it indicated a breakdown in the chain of command. We would then search for the source of the breakdown.

There were many other leadership techniques that he instituted during that tour at Fort Hood that are in use yet today. Later, after he retired, he wrote about them in a publication called *A Military Leadership Notebook: Principles into Practice.* Also, as a retired senior LTG, he performed leadership-based, special projects for the Army chief of staff.

Fig. 5 Jim as DCG

My tasking as the deputy commanding general (DCG, Figure 5) involved coordinating the activities of the non-divisional units at Fort Hood: a military police brigade, a signal brigade, a military intelligence brigade, an engineer brigade and an air cavalry brigade, plus an installation staff, as well as the two armored divisions. At that time there were approximately 45,000 soldiers, in addition to their dependents and many civilian employees. It goes without saying, it was a large installation.

We participated in numerous NATO REFORGER exercises. Our war plans at that time during the Cold War were for U.S.-based units to rapidly reinforce units already in Germany. We had prepositioned necessary equipment in German staging areas. The U.S.-based units would be flown over to Germany to sites near their prepositioned equipment, man the equipment and then be ready for battle. Thus, one of my additional jobs, which required frequent trips to Germany, was to organize and direct the activities of our forward III Corps HQ in Germany that would command the deployed units.

Initially, in Germany, I relied on local interpreters during my coordination with mostly German NATO officials, both military and civilian.

Our forward HQ was located near Muenster in North Germany, which was also near the German Armor School. When I traveled to Germany, proper protocol required me to make courtesy visits to the city government of Muenster, as well as the Armor School.

After several awkward visits with poor interpreters, I decided to make a change. I was authorized a captain as an aide, so I asked for volunteers from the various units at Fort Hood, which is normally the way a higher HQ asks for support from a lower HQ. My executive officer and I interviewed a number of officers who volunteered for the job, but one really stood out; a female military intelligence captain named Barbara Fast. She turned out to be perfect for the job.

Barbara had an outstanding background in military intelligence, including platoon and company command. She had a stable family (a supportive civilian husband and no children), was very athletic and was a linguist. She had studied at the Goethe Institute in Germany and was fluent in German. Captain Fast was definitely a front runner. This was demonstrated much later when as an MG, she would serve in Iraq and still later command the Military Intelligence School at Fort Huachuca, Arizona. When she retired, she became director of security for The Boeing Company.

Female aides were something new for Army general officers. Several females had been aides to Navy admirals by this time, but the Army had not yet bridged the gender gap. When I told Walt Ulmer that I would like to have Barbara for an aide, he thought for a minute and said that "this just might be the time to put our money where our mouth is."

We had had several occasions where we had to make judgment decisions regarding the feasibility of deploying female soldiers into countries where they might be vulnerable to sexual abuse. To avoid any question of impropriety, we went through a rather elaborate interview process that included Judy, and Barbara's husband, Paul, during which we established various ground rules, such as we would never be alone together. Whatever we were doing, we would always have a third party involved. It worked well. As a result of this, I probably became the first Army general officer to have a female aide.

In addition to coordinating my daily activities, Barbara always accompanied me on trips. In those days, I would jog 2 miles every day, even on overseas trips. When we were overseas, Barbara and a security officer would always jog along with me. Initially, when I would visit the German Armor School, the Germans were reluctant to have a female in the officers' club mess. I quickly established a policy of "No Captain Fast, No General Dozier." Before long, she charmed them all with her fluent German. And also, after a little while, I could have stayed at home as long as Barbara made the visit. The same approach worked with the mayor and city council of Muenster.

As alluded to earlier, there was one other incident regarding the deployment of females into risky sexual harassment areas. In the early 1980s, Fort Hood had the mission of supporting counterinsurgency operations in Central America. Our engineers were building airstrips in Honduras that would support our operations in El Salvador. We would deploy military police units to guard the perimeter gates in Honduras that protected the engineer units while they were working.

The working arrangement would be for a Honduran guard to be paired with one of our MPs. Initially, we deployed only males for this role. Then, we began to rethink the gender issue in the wake of "putting our money where our mouth was." On the next deployment, we included well-prepared females. Sure enough, on one occasion, a Honduran gate guard made a pass at one of our females. As the incident developed, she immediately notified her desk sergeant by radio. When the rapid response team got to the gate, she had already pretty well beat up the Honduran. That set the new standard. We had no further gender issues with regard to that particular mission.

American Academy of Achievement

Sometime around 1983–84, I was invited by the Army chief of staff to attend a session of the American Academy of Achievement (AAA) in New Orleans. Each year the Joint Chiefs of Staff would send notable members of the military to the annual gathering of the AAA, which was designed to bring together younger and older achievers so that they could share their thoughts, experiences and outlooks. I met such outstanding young achievers as Brooke Shields, Herschel Walker, plus an 11-year-old who was playing mind games with the nuclear physicist Edward Teller and winning most of the time.

Each of the older achievers in attendance was asked to give short talks about what had motivated them. The younger achievers would explain what was currently motivating them to do such great things. As the younger achievers began talking about their motivations, there seemed to be three major themes that began filtering through:

- Each of them expressed strong patriotism and a love for our country, especially with the opportunities that our free, risk-taking society had afforded them.

- They also felt that they had a special relationship with God. They believed that God had put them here for some purpose and that their primary quest was to fulfill that purpose.

- They all felt that they should always pursue excellence: that whatever one was doing, it was done to the very best of one's ability. Doing just enough to get by was not part of their psychological outlook.

That experience was a real eye-opener for me. It reinforced some of my own views and added others. It also provided an encouraging outlook regarding the future of our country.

Nearing the End

In early 1985, events beyond our control would soon determine the future military careers of both LTG Ulmer and me. The Cold War was winding down, but the Middle East was heating up in the wake of the 1979 overthrow of the Shah in Iran and the taking of U.S. hostages in the former U.S. Embassy in Tehran. After our abortive rescue attempt to secure the hostages, DOD placed major emphasis on the leadership, reorganization and training of our special operations forces. Thus, there was renewed emphasis on what was called the "Light Force," primarily infantry, airborne and special operations units. Military units of all the armed forces were faced with a new dynamic.

LTG Ulmer and I were part of what was then called the "Heavy Force." We were part of armor units, tailored to fight the heavily armored forces of the Warsaw Pact. Reflecting the new dynamic, the hierarchy of the Army soon changed, with general officers from the Light Force moving into senior leadership positions. General Wickham, an infantry careerist, replaced General Shy Meyer as Army chief of staff. This produced a cascade effect in the chain of command.

LTG Ulmer had been led to believe that he would be the next 4-star CG of Forces Command (FORSCOM), the next higher HQ to Fort Hood. I had been led to believe that I would soon become a division CG. Soon, an infantry MG was given command of an armored division at Fort Hood, traditionally an armored MG posting. As it turned out, this was done for him to gain experience for a later posting in the leadership of the Special Operations community. Our mentor at FORSCOM, General Cavazos, was replaced by a Light Force general, not LTG Ulmer. General Ulmer decided to retire, even though he was offered a 4-star position with NATO.

The handwriting was on the wall; since our prospects for further advancement were rather bleak, it was time to leave the Army. LTG Ulmer retired before I did, though I had a hand in helping him find a post-retirement job. Early in 1985, I had received a letter from the Center for Creative Leadership (CCL) in Greensboro, North Carolina. They were looking for a new president. They previously had good experiences with the military and were contacting previous graduates, such as me, seeking recommendations for a new president. I had attended one of their leadership development courses right after I was selected for promotion to BG.

At that time, the military services were sending all of their new flag officers to CCL. The course I attended after my selection as brigadier general was designed to give new flag officers a look at themselves through the eyes of others. Newly minted flag officers are pretty cocky and proud of themselves, but the military felt that they should be aware that "what you see in the mirror is not necessarily what others see." That course stood me in good stead later when I was a captive of the Red Brigades, in that always in the back of my mind, I made a special effort to tailor my actions with a view as to how they might appear to my captors.

Since LTG Ulmer and I lived across the street from one another, I took the letter from CCL over to him and asked what he thought. He seemed interested and told me to go ahead and recommend him. To make a long story short, I strongly recommended him for the president's position. After a series of interviews, he was accepted for the job. After we had both retired, he and I later collaborated on CCL projects for several years.

Once I had decided to retire, I decided not to be a "Beltway Bandit," a retired military person who would go to work for the defense industry, either within a company, or as a lobbyist in the Washington area. Once my retirement became known (Figure 6), I received some rather lucrative offers from the beltway sources. Instead, I decided to strike out on my own, so I contacted my former subordinate Dick Sklar, who had been my XO when I was a brigade com-

Fig. 6 Jim's retirement ceremony with LTG Saint

mander. Dick had retired earlier and was working in New York City in the information technology department of the Equitable Insurance Company. He introduced me to several headhunters who generated some tempting offers.

While all of this was going on, I received two offers which provided better fits. One was from the president of Norwich University in Northfield, Vermont, MG (Ret) Russ Todd. MG Todd had been the CG of the 1st Cavalry Division at Fort Hood when MG Patton was CG of the 2nd Armored Division and I was a brigade commander. MG (Ret) Jim Galloway, Todd's commandant of cadets, wanted to retire. This was the same Jim Galloway who had been CG of the 1st Armored Division when I called off the IG inspection of the 1-1 Cav, when I was a squadron commander.

The other job was generated by a former armor officer I had known, BG (Ret) Bill Rousse, who by this time was CEO of American Agronomics, a vertically integrated citrus processing company that grew citrus, processed it and then bottled the juice. He asked me to consider being the president of Golden Groves, one of American Agronomics' subsidiary companies. Golden Groves was a citrus grove management company whose headquarters was just outside my hometown of Arcadia, Florida. I first interviewed for the Norwich job in February, 1985.

I asked George Patton for advice about both jobs, and he answered that he would not advise me either way, since both would be challenging jobs. But like I mentioned earlier, he went on to say that if I urinated in the backyard of my house in Northfield, Vermont at 2 a.m., the whole town would be talking about it at breakfast that same day. That, coupled with the rigors of New England winters, made for an easy choice. I accepted the job in my home town, the comparatively balmy Arcadia, Florida. That decision opened a whole new career in agriculture, one which I have pursued ever since.

LTG Ulmer was replaced as CG of III Corps by newly promoted LTG Crosby (Butch) Saint. Butch and I had been in the same cadet company at West Point. Butch presided over my retirement ceremony and would later become a 4-star general and CINC of U.S. Army Europe (USAREUR).

After 35 years of military service, I retired from the Army, effective August 1, 1985. Some of my military friends had a cartoonist put together this picture, which showed my interest in the orange industry (Figure 7).

Fig. 7 Jim in the orange business

CHAPTER 9

Post-Military Careers

Security Consulting

After Army retirement, as a sideline, I began security consulting, based on contacts made while in the military. For instance, while at Fort Knox, I developed long standing relationships with various DOD schools that taught survival techniques and personal security. I taught classes at the USAF, U.S. Army Special Forces and the U.S. Army Aviation Center SERE (Survival, Evade, Resist, Escape) schools. However, the most enduring relationship was with the USAF Special Operations University DIT (Dynamics of International Terrorism) course. Judy and I taught at the USAF Special Operations School at Hurlburt Field, just outside of Fort Walton Beach, Florida, in Florida's panhandle. Judy and I started there in 1983. Judy left the course in 1998 due to health reasons, but our daughter, Cheryl, who had been with Judy during the kidnapping, replaced her. Due to age, I finally resigned from their faculty in 2015.

The DIT course is designed to better prepare mid-level leaders, both officer and enlisted, for assignments in international high-risk areas. It is one of the military's superb schools that trains our personnel for dangerous missions. It is a weeklong course that teaches the theory of terrorism and who the current actors are. There are also classes on personal security and cross-cultural relations. In our two-hour block, I focused on kidnapping

Fig. 1 Special Operations School Gunnery and Explosives Range

avoidance and kidnapping survival. Judy talked about the family aspects of such an event, which often eclipses the news surrounding the person kidnapped, because the media will always have access to the family.

The DIT course also traveled quite a bit. Depending on what was happening in various theaters, sometimes we would take the course to where the students were. This would be instead of taking them away from their commands to travel to Hurlburt. Over the course of my more than 30 years with the course, we traveled to the U.K., Germany, Italy, Korea, Hawaii and various military posts in the continental U.S. We also conducted the course for numerous civilian as well as military security and law enforcement groups in the U.S. To celebrate our 20 years with the DIT course, the USAF Special Operations School named their gunnery and explosives range after Judy and me (Figure 1).

After I retired, we continued with the Jim and Judy show for several years with various civilian audiences, until Judy's health began to deteriorate in 1998.

For several years I had a contract as a security advisor to the Deloitte Touche security department. I also spoke on national security issues quite frequently at various symposia as a representative of the Fairfax Group.

Although I no longer work for Deloitte, I still frequently present talks about national security issues.

Other Civilian Employment

Judy and I started planning our move to Florida as soon as I accepted the job with Golden Groves. Since we enjoyed boating, we both wanted to live near the Gulf of Mexico, a small boater's paradise. Since Arcadia is inland from the Gulf, we drew a one-hour commuting arc from Arcadia, which intersected the Gulf of Mexico coast, just north of Sarasota, to the north, and in the south, just south of Fort Myers. We then contacted a relocation agency in Washington, D.C., run by a friend of ours, who set up appointments with realtors along the Gulf Coast. We looked at numerous waterfront properties from Sarasota down to Fort Myers. We finally settled on a four-bedroom house on an inlet at the mouth of Daughtry's Creek, which flowed into the Caloosahatchee River in North Fort Myers, and then to the Gulf of Mexico.

The house we selected was chosen with the expectation of Judy's parents spending their winters with us. The structure was U-shaped, with a swimming pool between the two arms of the U. One arm contained two bathrooms and three bedrooms, one of which could be made into a studio for Judy's dad, an artist. At the base of the U was located the kitchen, dining room and living room. The other arm of the U contained a main bedroom, bath, dressing room and a large family room, which overlooked a large wooden deck and dock. The house was about 20 years old, so we set about remodeling it.

Remodeling the house gave me my first experience with civilian bureaucracy. We hired an architect and contractor. After we worked out the plans, our contractor applied for a building permit from the Lee County Permitting Office. It was turned down. It seemed the previous owner, a local banker, had done some unpermitted construction, which was discovered by a building inspector about the time we bought the house. I visited the county permitting office and discussed the issue, initially with a clerk. She was no help at all, so I asked to talk to her boss.

I told both ladies that I would gladly bring all of the unpermitted construction up to code if necessary. They wouldn't buy that and insisted that I tear out all of the unpermitted work before they would issue a permit. This would involve considerable work, which would have greatly added to the cost of the renovation. I was stymied.

Fortunately, I had a neighbor, a fellow Rotarian, who was chairman of the board of SW Florida Goodwill Industries. Hatton Rogers was a retired Nestlé executive who had many dealings with local bureaucrats. A side issue, which didn't help matters, was that during the previous year, four of our five Lee County commissioners had been indicted for various reasons and had been replaced. As a result, county government was in a state of turmoil. By the way, Rotarians have some pretty darn good guidelines for the "things we think, say and do." They go like this, known as the Rotary Four-Way Test:

- Is it the truth?
- Will it build goodwill and better friendships?
- Will it be fair to all concerned?
- Will it be beneficial to all concerned?

If so, "live it."

As an example of the moral ramifications of these guidelines, in 2019, we persuaded a member of our Rotary club, a reserve Army officer, to resign from the club due to some of his campaign ads that violated the Rotary Four-Way Test. He was a lawyer running for state attorney, and with regard to allegations toward his campaign opponent, he was intellectually dishonest.

As to our difficulties with our building permit, Hatt (Figure 2) suggested that he discuss my permit problem with one of the then current county commissioners, who was also a Rotarian. I readily agreed. A short time later, I received a call from Commissioner Roland Eastwood, who told me that my building permit was ready. I thanked him and went to the permitting office to get the permit. I waited in the lobby until my name was called and was then ushered into the office of the lady who had previously denied my permit. She was sitting behind an absolutely clean desk with my permit sitting right in the middle of it. As I approached her desk, she stood up, grabbed the permit and said: "HERE," then walked

Fig. 2 Jim with Hatt Rogers

Fig. 3 Hatt and Peggy Rogers

out of the office without another word. Her fiefdom had been overturned by the commissioner.

Hatton Rogers also introduced me to a nonpartisan political organization called BUPAC (**B**usiness people **U**nited for **P**olitical **A**ction **C**ommittee). This was a small business political action committee (PAC) that was organized to promote good government in the wake of the previously mentioned indictment of the four county commissioners. When I first joined BUPAC in 1985, it consisted of about 10–15 people, usually small-business owners, who would get together for breakfast meetings. From time to time, we would invite candidates for local elected county offices (usually school board and county commission) to speak about local issues. In some cases, we would actively recruit promising candidates.

The organization has grown over the years and the roster now numbers over a hundred people. It has morphed into a very influential local political organization. We endorse candidates and support the campaigns of those we endorse with campaign contributions. I have been BUPAC's chair several times and have thoroughly enjoyed being involved in local politics. In the nonelection years, we solicit speakers who talk about subjects that we know will be issues in the next year's political campaigns. As a result, when the following year's candidates speak, we often know more about the issues than they do. BUPAC is now viewed as a tough, but educational, group for prospective candidates and their knowledge of the issues.

Unknown to me at the time, Hatt and his wife, Peggy (Figure 3), would continue to play a role in my future life.

Golden Groves

Starting in Fall 1985, my job as president of Golden Groves got me pretty deeply involved in the Florida citrus industry. Golden Groves was the citrus caretaker and grower relations arm of Orange-Co, a vertically integrated citrus company headquartered in Tampa. In addition to Golden Groves, Orange-Co also operated a frozen citrus juice concentration plant (also near Arcadia) and a bottling company near Tampa. Harold Holder, the owner of American Agronomics, and Bill Rousse, the CEO, introduced me to most of the key players in the Florida citrus industry, both large and small. I found it to be a fascinating industry, composed of growers, harvesters, processors and marketers. Most large companies are vertically integrated, lumping all of the functions under one large roof. However, there are still many small businesses in the industry that occupy specialty niches, such as growing, harvesting, marketing, caretaking, irrigation, retail sales, etc.

I also became involved with several of the University of Florida agricultural research organizations, such as the Institute of Food and Agricultural Sciences (IFAS) and the U.S. Department of Agriculture (USDA) citrus research stations.

When he hired me, Bill Rousse had asked me to tighten up the operations of Golden Groves. It had been poorly led and its integration into the overall vertically integrated Orange-Co business was not up to par.

This was to be my first civilian experience with turning around an organization. It would not be the last.

Fortunately, most of the employees were dedicated people who wanted to do a good job. It was shades of commanding 1-1 Cavalry all over again. In addition, a number of employees had been students, or had relatives who had been students of my mother's, a teacher at the DeSoto County High School for nearly 40 years. I also knew some of them from high school days.

I convinced Bill Rousse that I would benefit from what in the military is called a Transition Team—a small group of two to three people that would conduct interviews and do surveys of all elements of the organization. Two friends from the military had retired by this time and had formed their own company, so I hired them to do the work. The process took about two weeks, but was very informative.

While all this was going on, I struck out on my own, learning everything I could about the organization. I started by visiting and chatting with the several hundred employees who made up each element of the company, including office staff, caretaking and harvesting personnel, maintenance department, truck drivers, etc.

The most important thing that we learned from the Transition Team and my visits was a lack of effective communication between various elements of Golden Groves. Bill Rousse had hit the nail on the head by replacing the previous CEO, a micromanager who was loath to delegate. The team also discovered that there was a definite lack of communication between other elements of Orange-Co.

Once we found out what the problems were, we went about fixing them.

I started a weekly staff meeting with all department heads. At first, this was a little awkward in that staff heads were reluctant to put their particular problems on the table. That quickly disappeared, though, once they realized that doing this would solve said problems. Staff meetings then became very productive. After several months, key staff members told me that they were now effectively coordinating with each other and asked if we could reduce the frequency of the weekly staff meetings. I agreed!

Bill Rousse also started holding bi-weekly meetings between Orange-Co key personnel and those key people in our frozen citrus concentration plant. That pretty well solved our communication problems.

Citrus Freezes

When I arrived at Golden Groves in the fall of 1985, the industry was recovering from a series of devastating freezes that had killed large numbers of citrus trees, particularly in the center of the state. A large part of that damaged acreage was not redeveloped for citrus, but was instead sold to housing developers. What once were citrus groves along U.S. Route 27, running north to south through the center of the state, were now devoted to one housing development after another. Orange-Co was damaged in 1985, but not devastated.

To put freezes into perspective, in the latter part of the 19th century, the citrus industry in Florida first was established in north Florida, near

Jacksonville. Successive freezes kept moving the industry further south. That process is still continuing. Right now, the industry is concentrated in the counties south of Interstate Route 4 and also along the east coast, which is warmed by the Gulf Stream. So much for global warming.

In 1985, Orange-Co was rebuilding, removing dead trees from groves, starting our own greenhouses to produce resets (small new citrus trees to replace those killed by the freezes), and dealing with reduced input to our frozen concentrate plants.

On Friday, December 28, 1986, Florida was hit by another severe freeze. We knew it was coming and had taken what precautions we could. This included raising water in the irrigation ditches to create small micro-environments. We protected our greenhouse operations with micro-sprinklers that would spray 73°F well water, thus releasing heat inside of the structures to keep the resets from damage. We were mostly successful.

As a sidebar, on that late December morning, I was in my office, the back door of which opened onto to our maintenance department. I heard a frantic knock on the door. I opened the door and there stood the maintenance manager, whom I had known from high school days:

He said, "Jimmy, Jimmy come look. The space shuttle just blowed up." I went outside and looked up to see the multiple contrails of the shuttle debris. It turned out the freezing weather had affected some devices on the shuttle, which caused them to fail, creating the tragedy. It was a sobering, gut wrenching moment.

Orange-Co recovered fairly rapidly after the 1986 freeze and our 1987 citrus production considerably improved.

In early summer of 1987, Bill Rousse flew over from Tampa to Arcadia to have a private chat. Bill had been a helicopter pilot in the military and thus was able to fly a leased helicopter on business trips. He stated that Harold Holder was in negotiations to sell Golden Groves to Procter and Gamble and that he expected it to happen very quickly. As it turned out, he was right on target. Once the sale was agreed upon, the Florida manager of Procter and Gamble came over to discuss personnel changes. He told me right up front that he was going to flatten the organization and that I would be let go. We discussed personnel and how best to go about his intended reorganization. I made several suggestions and he eventually agreed to my recommended reorganization. I left Orange-Co in late summer of 1987. However, by this time I had bought 50 acres of citrus groves in the Golden Groves complex that I would profitably operate until tornadoes associated with Hurricane Charlie flattened them in 2004.

Sun Coast Media Group

News of my departure from Golden Groves traveled quickly in DeSoto County, and soon after, I received several possible employment offers. The most interesting came from the publisher, Derrick Dunn-Rankin, of the Sun Coast Media Group (SCMG), the parent company of one of Arcadia's two weekly newspapers. He came to Arcadia to interview me. He said that he needed someone like me to help organize the conversion of some of his publications from weekly to daily editions. I, of course, told him I knew nothing about what he was asking me to do. He responded that he needed someone with organizational and leadership skills, and that he would teach me the technicalities of the job. In addition, he wanted me to be a troubleshooter for the SCMG. After discussing the offer with Judy, I accepted.

The Sun Coast Media Group was headquartered in Venice, Florida, about an hour away by car from Fort Myers. In addition to its daily publication in Venice, the *Venice Gondolier*, it had weekly publications in nearby Englewood, North Port, Port Charlotte, Sarasota and Arcadia. North of Tampa, in Hernando County, there also were two weekly publications. These were the ones Derrick wanted to convert to daily publications, so as to compete with the Tampa and St. Petersburg dailies. Supporting the various publications were three printing plants located in Venice, Charlotte Harbor and Hernando County. The plants in Venice and Charlotte Harbor were linked electronically so that one could pinch-hit for the other, depending on the printing load.

Interestingly, one of my first tasks for the SCMG was to arrange for the installation of lightning protection for the printing plants. Just before my arrival, lightning had knocked out the link between the Venice and Charlotte Harbor plants. Derrick had a friend who was an expert on lightning protection. He was also a private pilot who flew down to meet with me. He designed a protection system and I arranged for a contractor to install it, which solved the problem.

Derrick and I made numerous trips to Hernando County to start the transition process. My learning curve was very steep. The dynamics of all facets of publishing a newspaper: newsroom, distribution, advertising, etc., shifted into high gear. This called for staff increases as well as staff reorganization. By the time I left SCMG in the summer of 1988, the process was well underway and was eventually successful. My time with them was one of the most interesting periods in my post-retirement endeavors.

CHAPTER 10

Congressional Campaign, Other Work, and Loss of Judy

In late 1987, our congressman, Connie Mack III, grandson of the baseball great, announced that he would run for the U.S. Senate, hoping to be one of Florida's two senators. He and I had become rather close friends through my efforts as a member of his Service Academy Nominating Committee. I also had helped him campaign in a previous election. In early 1988, he asked if I would consider running to replace him. I was flattered. He said that he could not publicly support me, but that he would recommend one of his previous campaign managers, Tricia Molzow, to work with me. His district was a large one, comprising most of coastal Southwest Florida. It stretched from Sarasota in the north, down through Naples in the south.

I discussed this possibility with Judy and a circle of very close friends. I received all kinds of advice, ranging from "don't touch this with a 10-foot pole" to "give it a go." In the meantime, I attended a campaign school in Washington, D.C., run by the Republican National Committee. I also discussed the possibility with Derrick Dunn-Rankin, my boss at the SCMG. Derrick had his ear to the ground in the district and he pointed out that since a candidate would be running for an open seat, there would be many people who would like the job.

Trish Molzow suggested that we commission a polling organization to do a survey to see if there would be enough support if I did decide to run. I paid for the survey out of my own pocket and it showed that I had a very good chance of being elected. Regretfully, the survey was done before all of the contenders had entered the race.

After a great deal of further advice and consideration, I decided to run and resigned from my job with the SCMG.

Little did I realize at the time that this would be some of the hardest work I would ever have to do. I now have a profound respect for anyone, in any party, who seeks public office. It is an arduous task.

Trish helped me put a campaign organization together. I hired a campaign manager to do the everyday work, a young man I had met in campaign school, who had managed a prior campaign in New England. Trish remained the overall campaign strategist. We fleshed out the team with friends who would be responsible for financial reporting and fund-raising. We also put together a small office staff in an office building donated by another friend.

I outfitted one of our automobiles, a Honda Civic, with a portable telephone and hit the road. Trish and my campaign manager put together an issue list and I started to bone up on them. In 1988, there weren't a lot of national issues on which folks in Southwest Florida were interested. Most of the issues were local. I spoke several times a day to women's clubs and political organizations, and as more candidates joined the race, candidate forums. I always closed my remarks with, "You can always depend on me for straight talk and honest answers."

Initially, I was the main candidate in the race and attracted quite a bit of attention. Then the inevitable happened, just like Derrick Dunn-Rankin had predicted: Two powerful, popular politicians entered the race. The first to enter was Porter Goss, a former CIA official and a very popular Lee County commissioner, who previously had been mayor of Sanibel. The second, a month or so later, was Skip Bafalis, who had previously lost the seat to Connie Mack. Their entry changed the dynamics of the race. Both were well-funded and began to run TV ads. I was not well-funded and could not respond in kind.

Nevertheless, when the votes were counted after the Republican primary election, I came in third with 18% of the vote. Since neither Goss nor Bafalis had received a plurality in the primary election, a runoff was required. Both asked for my support. During the campaigning, Judy and I had gotten to know the Goss' very well. Even though we were political opponents, we remained close friends and conducted our campaigns without criticizing each other. Judy and I decided to support Porter Goss, much to the consternation of Bafalis. Porter was elected and served with distinction for a number of terms until he was appointed to head the CIA by President George W. Bush.

I learned a lot about politics by being a candidate and I have been active in Republican politics ever since.

Service Academy Nominating Committee

After retiring from the Army in 1985, I had made a mental note that if I ever had the chance, I would try to do something about the problems with the service academy appointment process. That chance came several years later. Our congressman at the time, Connie Mack, invited me to sit on his service academy nominating panel, which was made up of five to seven members of his constituency, who interviewed prospective nominees. Connie insisted that politics not be considered in the selection process. A year or so later, when I became chair of the panel, Porter Goss, who succeeded Mack as congressman, asked us to develop metrics that would substantiate the panel decisions. This would help him with constituents who asked for favors.

As a result, we developed a scoring system that measured the "whole person," as requested by the academies themselves. Our scoring system incorporated an applicant's grade point average, SAT scores, athletic participation, community involvement and leadership experience, plus the gut feeling of each interviewer. The resulting scores were fed into a computer program that would print out an order of merit list for each academy. The congressman would then skim his nominations right off the top of the respective lists. He then had a document on which he based his answers to constituent's requests for special consideration.

Each year we would have parents tell us that they didn't know about service college opportunities. We heard the phrase, "If we had only known" many times. Thus, in an effort to inform parents of high school juniors about career opportunities in the military services, we began what we called Academy Day. Academy Day seemed to solve this problem. This was a half-day session at a local college that included the congressman, who emphasized the non-political nature of our system, and a serving cadet/midshipman from each academy. Also included were the academy liaison officers and selectees from the prior year. We described in detail the nominating process to include our scoring system. Since then, Academy Day has significantly cut down the number of political inquiries/requests received by the congressman's office.

Thus, another successful turnaround effort.

David C. Brown Farms

One of my supporters during my congressional campaign, along with his father, a former Collier County commissioner, was Dr. David C. Brown, a well-known local ophthalmologist who was CEO of Eye Centers of Florida, a vertically integrated eye care business. He and his father had been very generous in their financial support of my campaign.

After I lost in the primary in 1988, I received a phone call from Dr. Brown's chief financial officer, Gary Delanous, asking if I would consider joining Dr. Brown's team. Dr. Brown was in the process of organizing and expanding his father's (who was not well and wanted to retire) agricultural operations. Gary said that the organization would be called David C. Brown Farms and the position would involve pulling the various agricultural businesses together into an integrated whole. It sounded like a task that I would enjoy. After further discussion with Gary and Judy, I accepted Dr. Brown's offer and went right to work.

Although my office was in South Fort Myers, co-located with Gary and his financial management staff, my responsibilities would range over five southwestern Florida counties. Dr. Brown and his family owned cattle ranches in Hardee and DeSoto counties, where they produced a breed of purebred cattle called Beefmaster. These cattle were sturdy, much sought after animals for beef production. The ranch in DeSoto County actually straddled the DeSoto-Charlotte county line. They also owned citrus groves in Collier County. I would later establish a citrus grove and a vegetable farm on acreage adjacent to his DeSoto-Charlotte property. The family also grew winter vegetables (mainly tomatoes, cucumbers and peppers) on farms at several locations in Collier and DeSoto counties. All told, Dr. Brown and his family had agricultural operations, which included two ranches, six citrus groves, nine farms and a packing house, sitting on approximately 6,000 acres.

The Beefmaster cattle at Dr. Brown's ranches mainly produced embryos and semen, which were sold to other ranchers to improve the bloodlines of their beef cattle. We sold very few actual animals. Several times a year, we would fly to cattle sales in various parts of the South, where other Beefmaster owners would buy and sell animals.

I had another steep learning curve as I became ever more involved in Dr. Brown's various agricultural businesses. It became, however, one of the more enjoyable, professionally rewarding times in my life. It also opened doors that increased my knowledge of agriculture.

One of my first tasks was to further vertically integrate his winter vegetable business. I had a vegetable packing house built at the farmer's market in Immokalee, a hub of the winter vegetable business in Southwest Florida. We worked out an agreement with the state of Florida, whereby we could operate the packing house rent free at the farmer's market if we would pay for its construction. It took about a year to get it built, the packing lines installed and a manager hired. We also established a sales office in the packing house and hired a salesman/vegetable broker. I established my own alternate office at the packing house as well.

Dr. Brown was a hands-on owner and also an accomplished helicopter pilot. Twice a week, Wednesday afternoons and all day Saturday, we would get in his helicopter, which he personally piloted, and visit his various operations. I would make sure that the right person was at each site to bring him up to speed on what was going on there. When we landed at each location, we would be met by the person in charge and we would tour the property in a pickup truck.

I also became more involved with the University of Florida Institute of Food and Agricultural Science (IFAS), which had a citrus and vegetable research station near Immokalee. For several years, and since I had a strong background in citrus by this time, I chaired the IFAS Citrus Research Advisory Committee. I also, in conjunction with *Citrus Industry* magazine, helped establish the annual Citrus Exposition in Fort Myers, which brought vendors and citrus growing owners together. The Citrus Expo, as it became known, exists to this day.

At the request of other vegetable brokers, Dr. Brown also explored the possibility of establishing farms in Guatemala and the Dominican Republic. Dr. Brown owned a business jet which we would use for such trips. After giving the opportunities serious thought, we decided not to branch out that far, mainly because the infrastructure and political situations in those countries would not support the movement of product from field to ports/airports.

Dr. Brown also expressed an interest in aquaculture. We used his jet to visit catfish farms and processing facilities in Mississippi and Arkansas.

During one such visit, we met a woman, who at that time, from a catfish farmer's point of view, was the most important woman in Mississippi. She was the taster at a catfish processing plant we were visiting. When a catfish farmer drove his tank truck up to the entrance gate, this lady would dip a fish out of the tank truck with a net, chop it up and put the pieces in a microwave oven. She would then taste the results for flavor. Since catfish are bottom feeders, they would sometimes go off-taste due to their environment, so catfish farmers tried to feed them floating pellets to compensate, which also increased protein levels and fat. If she gave the farmer a "thumbs up" after her taste test, you could see the sweat dry up on his or her face. If she gave him a "thumbs down," he would drive off, to better feed the fish and try again.

We became fascinated by the industry and came very close to leasing the Seminole Indian catfish farm. We ultimately decided not to do so as that facility was very rundown and would have required quite a bit of investment to be competitive. We then took a look at raising tilapia, a farm-raised fish that was becoming popular at about that time. We decided to put together an experimental farm.

An interesting incident occurred while I was getting the permits for the experimental farm. I had a run-in with environmental activists. I had secured federal and state permits, but when I applied for the Collier County permit, it was denied due to an ordinance that environmentalists had helped enact forbidding non-native plants and animals from being introduced into Collier County. This was surprising in that almost every body of fresh water (ponds, streams, ditches, etc.) contained tilapia, whose eggs were distributed by birds and animals. I finally took a member of the permitting office out to see what Mother Nature had done. The county eventually modified the ordinance.

Even though I finally secured all the necessary permits for the experimental tilapia farm, we never built it. Regretfully, Dr. Brown had expanded his other businesses (mainly aircraft leasing) too fast and had to declare bankruptcy. I was let go in early 1993 and he shut down the agribusinesses a short time later.

In Business for Myself

By the time I left Dr. Brown in 1993, I was thoroughly hooked on agriculture. I looked around for something to do that was agriculturally related. I explored several possibilities, including a hardware store that provided specialty parts to boaters and agricultural growers. During this process, a man named Roger Custer, whom I had met at an aquaculture conference a year or so earlier, invited me to visit his 10-acre tropical foliage plant operation on nearby Pine Island. He was growing several varieties of crotons, a colorful tropical plant.

Roger was growing on contract for several large nurseries. He told me he needed capital to expand his operation and asked if I was interested in a partnership. I gave it some thought and discussed it with Judy; after visiting some of Roger's customers, it appeared to be a stable business, so we decided to give it a try. The partnership got off to a good start, but I soon came to realize that Roger had some controlling personality issues that made getting along with him difficult.

Also, by this time, our son, Scott, had been discharged from the Coast Guard. After working and going to school in northwest Florida, he decided to move to Fort Myers. Scott seemed interested in agriculture, so I put him to work at the Pine Island nursery. He immediately became enamored with agriculture. Unfortunately, Roger viewed the father-son relationship as a threat to the partnership, in that Scott was becoming more and more involved in the growing, marketing and delivery of our product. It soon became evident that the partnership with Custer was not going to continue to work, so I offered to buy Roger out. He reluctantly agreed. For several years, Scott and I successfully operated the nursery and expanded our list of customers.

As previously mentioned, while at Golden Groves, I had purchased 50 acres of orange groves and had been paying someone else to take care of the acreage. They were paying a nice return on my investment. We were thus involved in two separate agricultural operations, some 70 miles apart. In 1995 we decided to consolidate both operations at the orange grove near Arcadia. That would allow us to use some of the same equipment for both the nursery and the orange grove and do our own citrus management. I bought a small tractor that would allow us to do our own citrus caretaking. I had previously arranged with a high school friend for him to harvest the citrus crop.

The decision turned out to be a good one. I converted three acres of orange grove into shade houses, dug three wells for irrigation, moved the nursery operation into the citrus grove property and sold the Pine Island property. We continued to successfully operate the businesses until 2004, when as previously mentioned, a tornado, spawned by Hurricane Charlie, flattened both the citrus grove and the foliage plant shade house structures.

I philosophically looked at this as Divine Intervention. About this time, a very virulent citrus disease began to affect the citrus industry, so it really was a good time to get out of the business. I decided to really retire this time and devote my time to community work and care of Judy.

Loss of Judy

Judy's death capped a long illness. In the late 1990s I noticed that she began to move more slowly through airports. Since she was a smoker, I initially thought that she was stopping in the smoking areas while I went on ahead to the gates to get ready to board with our carry-on items. However, in late 1998, she froze on stage during a DIT presentation in San Diego and had trouble recovering. It finally dawned on me that she had a more serious condition. An examination by a neurologist was inconclusive. Several months later she fell while taking a shower and suffered a severe
laceration on her head. I could not stop the bleeding, so I took her to the emergency room at Southwest Regional Medical Center in Fort Myers.

The emergency room personnel during their examinations discovered a suspicious area in her brain. A neurosurgeon confirmed that it was a metastasized lung cancer that had gone to the brain. The neurosurgeon recommended radiation to shrink the brain tumor. This did not turn out well at all.

In the meantime, our friend Hatton Rogers contacted a member of the Moffitt Center Board of Directors in Tampa for Judy to be admitted to the hospital in order to address the lung cancer issue. The Moffitt Center is a world-renowned cancer center. After a complex series of tests, the Moffitt Center surgeons recommended removal of the lower lobe of her left lung, which was accomplished in short order. After another series of tests, the surgeon called me into his office and announced that Judy was among a very small number of lung cancer patients who were now cancer free. The operation had been successful.

Not so the radiation for the brain tumor. In those days, radiation treatments were not as precise as they now are. Even though the brain tumor was destroyed, the radiation also produced an edema in the surrounding tissue, which contributed to her infirmities and complicated a subsequent diagnosis of Parkinson's disease. It seemed she had developed Parkinson's early on, but the diagnosis was complicated by the edema associated with the radiation.

By this time, Judy required constant care. Initially, I hired someone to spend the day with her while I was away at work. Finally, I moved her into a skilled nursing facility in nearby Cape Coral. She died on August 27, 2005 in a hospice in Cape Coral. Losing Judy after 48 years of marriage was tough for me. Our love was profound; together we had been involved in so many adventures and had traveled the world. We had raised a family together. I depended on her for many, many things and her passing deeply impacted me.

CHAPTER II

Community Involvement

After I retired from the Army in 1985, I almost immediately became involved with the business, professional and political communities in several locations. Since I was initially working in Arcadia, which is in DeSoto County, I joined the Rotary Club there, along with several other civic organizations. Also, since I had relatives in Arcadia, I was often asked through them to relate my kidnapping experiences to various church and civic organizations.

The same was true in Fort Myers, which is in Lee County, two counties south of DeSoto. Judy and I were very active in the Republican Executive Committee in Lee County and we joined the Royal Palm Yacht Club in Fort Myers, a leading civic and social organization in the county. We also played very active roles in our local home owners' association.

Also, while working at Orange-Co, I became involved with some of the citrus-related activities throughout the state, particularly the annual Florida Citrus Expo, at that time sponsored by *Citrus Industry* magazine. The Expo was designed to bring together growers, vendors and researchers from the University of Florida Institute of Food and Agricultural Sciences (IFAS). In addition to facilitating vendors showing their wares, the researchers at IFAS would conduct seminars on various citrus related subjects. I was instrumental in getting the Expo relocated to the Lee County Civic Center, just north of Fort Myers.

After no longer working for Orange-Co and since now living in North Fort Myers, I transferred my Rotary membership from the Arcadia club to the North Fort Myers club. I would later transfer membership again to the Fort Myers Downtown Rotary Club, where I remain a member to this day. As previously mentioned, the values of Rotary have become very important in my life since leaving military service.

Lee County Electric Cooperative (LCEC)

In early 1993, Gary Delanous, Dr. Brown's CFO and C/S, said that Dr. Brown had been asked by the board chair of the Lee County Electric Cooperative (LCEC, an electric power distribution cooperative) if he would agree for me to join the LCEC board. Dr. Brown agreed and I began a 23-year relationship with one of the finest organizations of which I have ever been a member. It also began a relationship with the CEO, Pamela May (later Pamela Noland), and John Noland, corporate counsel. Pam resigned as CEO when she and John decided to marry. Being a board member began another steep learning curve, regarding the intricacies of the electric power industry.

After I had my feet on the ground at LCEC, I was appointed as a representative to "Statewide," an organization of all of Florida's electric distribution co-ops. Later, I was appointed as our representative to Seminole Electric, a Generation and Transmission (G & T) co-op.

Following my marriage to Sharlene, I had to resign from the LCEC board in 2006, after moving out of the LCEC service area.

Little did I realize at the time that Pam and John Noland would become our very close friends.

Good Wheels

During the summer of 1996, Hatton Rogers called me with a special request. A mutual friend of ours, Marion Chambers, had called him regarding problems with the leadership of Good Wheels, a para-transit company that furnished transportation for the disadvantaged with state sponsored grants throughout five Southwest Florida counties. Marion was a member of the Good Wheels board of directors. Hatt thought I would be a good influence on the board.

Marion had told Hatt that the leadership of the company had become dysfunctional due to nepotism and corruption. The CEO had hired relatives for key jobs within the company. There also were several board members who had favoritism conflicts of interest by awarding contracts to friends without competitive bidding. I further discussed the matter with Marion and agreed to be a member of the board.

After attending several monthly board meetings, I found that Marion's concerns were well founded. I started asking board members questions regarding some of their decisions. This caused two board members to resign. More, including the board chairman, resigned later as I kept asking questions. As each resigned, I recruited business people from other boards of which I was a member to take their places. Pretty soon, those I had recruited became a majority on the board, and when the chairman resigned, I was elected chair.

Those I recruited included:

- Joe Slee, owner of a marine services company and a Rotarian.
- Alan Katzman, retired CEO of a large manufacturing organization and a Rotarian.
- Glee Duff, retired owner of a large advertising firm.
- Gary Bryant, retired U. S. Army LTC, who had recently rebuilt the Lee County JROTC program and a Rotarian.

A remaining member of the board was a CPA, whom I asked to take a good look at the financial records. She reported that they were a mess. As the new chairman, I asked the Florida Commission for the Disadvantaged to do a functional audit of the entire Good Wheels operation. The report that came back recommended significant leadership changes were in order. I discussed these with the CEO. She seemed reluctant to make them.

I then asked the board to consider replacing the CEO. They agreed and the operations director became the interim CEO.

Since he had gotten me involved with Good Wheels in the first place, I asked Hatt Rogers to chair a search committee for a new CEO. After interviewing numerous applicants, including board member Gary Bryant, he reported that he did not need to look any further. He recommended that we promote from within by selecting Gary as the new CEO.

The board quickly approved Gary as the new CEO. Gary would successfully lead Good Wheels for the next 14 years, turning it into one of the most successful businesses supporting the disadvantaged in the state.

I remained on the board as chairman and as a member of the board for nearly the next 20 years.

Lee County government left a lot to be desired in those days. When I moved to Lee County in 1985, four of the five county commissioners were under indictment for various reasons, and all were convicted. Later, the Lee County tax collector was indicted for cashing tax payment checks and putting the money in his personal account.

At that time, we made our tax payment checks payable to Dick Steele, tax collector, so it was easy for him to put some of the checks in his personal account. That system has now been changed, due partly to the efforts of BUPAC. Still, later in the early 1990s, another county commissioner was indicted for not paying his federal income tax and still another was indicted for corruption (influence peddling) involving her boyfriend. Still later, the son (also a county commissioner) of the county commissioner previously indicted for not paying his income tax, was indicted for involvement in a heroin sting. An additional county commissioner was also later indicted and convicted for influence peddling. Fortunately, we had a strong state attorney at the time, who expertly and expeditiously handled these rather sensitive cases.

I am very proud to state that BUPAC, which meets weekly, played an active role in seeking qualified replacements for all of those indicted, as well as those seeking public office in general. BUPAC to this day endorses and provides financial support to candidates that we feel are qualified. During the "off election" years, BUPAC invites speakers to talk about the issues in forthcoming elections, so that in the election years our members usually know more about the important issues than some of the candidates. BUPAC is viewed by aspiring candidates as a tough venue. BUPAC's efforts have been very successful. Candidates actively seek our support and those we have endorsed have performed reasonably well.

We now have good government throughout Lee County.

Sharlene

For some time after losing Judy, I was at loose ends. However, I quickly found out that being a widower in a relatively small part of Florida was very challenging. I received all sorts of advice from folks who had lost their spouses. One of the best was, "Beware of widows with casseroles." I was frequently invited to dinners and introduced to various divorcees and widows. On one occasion while at a high school reunion in Arcadia, I sat near a single high school classmate, several classes behind me, who insisted that we go to lunch. I reluctantly agreed. I had not known her very well way back then, but we decided to meet at a Cracker Barrel restaurant in Fort Myers. I arrived early and was sitting in a rocking chair at the front of the restaurant when the breeze blew a sickly sweet perfume my way. I looked up and coming out of the parking lot upwind was my high school classmate. That was the last time we saw each other.

I had previously mentioned how influential Hatton Rogers and his wife, Peg, were in my life. They had been watching the progress of me being a widower and didn't like what they saw, so they decided to get actively involved. I didn't know it at the time, but Peg had been involved in successful matchmaking on eight previous occasions. I was about to become her ninth project.

On May 18, 2006, the Rogers invited me to a dinner at their home, which was just down the street from mine, along with some mutual friends, Pamela and John Noland. At that time, Hatt was chairman of the board of Goodwill Industries of Southwest Florida. Shortly after we had agreed on the date for the dinner, Hatt called to say that since Goodwill had a board meeting that day, he was going to invite a member of the board, Sharlene Hamel, to join us. Peg by this time had told the Nolands what was going on and asked that they go home a bit early. I was left completely in the dark!

I had met Sharlene on several occasions, though I knew her husband much better, as he had been the mayor of Fort Myers. He also had been

Fig. 1 Jim and Sharlene

a former member of the Goodwill board, but had died in 2002. Sharlene then had taken his place on the Goodwill board.

We had cocktails and then a great time at the rather informal dinner. Shortly after dessert, the Nolands announced that they had better get home since John had a tough day coming up. That's when the match-making began (Figure 1). After we had chatted for a while following dessert, Peg and Hatt suggested that the four of us, on another day, go out to dinner at the Royal Palm Yacht Club, where we were all members. We talked about that for a bit, then Peg suggested that better yet, why don't Sharlene and I go to dinner somewhere by ourselves. Sharlene and I thought that was a good idea, so we settled on a date. In the meantime, Peg was busy emailing photos and stories about both of us to each other. Sharlene and I had several very enjoyable dinner dates before she left for North Carolina for the summer. She usually spent several months in her condo in Banner Elk, in the North Carolina mountains.

The Rogers also had a condo in nearby Blowing Rock. I had visited them there on several previous occasions. Hatt soon invited me up to visit again and suggested that if I wanted to spend some time with Shar-lene, there were several motels near Banner Elk that would be convenient. Since Sharlene and I had been conducting a rapidly developing romance via email, I readily took him up on his idea and contacted Sharlene. We spent a very enjoyable couple of days; however, I slept in her spare bed-room rather than in a motel.

Later that summer, I was involved in a leadership development program (Leadership During a Crisis) at the Center for Creative Leadership in Greensboro, North Carolina. I invited Sharlene to attend, so we spent several enjoyable days in Greensboro.

During that visit, Sharlene mentioned that she and her daughter, Laura, would soon be going on a tour to Italy. It just so happened that Cheryl, my daughter, and I were scheduled to go to Italy at the same time to again thank those who rescued me, as well as those who supported my family during my kidnapping. Cheryl and I changed our travel plan so that we could all meet in Montalcino, a small hilltop town in Tuscany, where Sharlene and Laura were staying for two weeks. Again, we had a great several days.

On a subsequent visit to Banner Elk that summer, I proposed marriage to Sharlene and she readily agreed. Sharlene set the date for December 1, 2006, her birthday. That certainly simplified my responsibility for remembering birthdays and anniversaries. We discussed our upcoming marriage plans with our children to include Sharlene's three children, Steve, Art and Laura (Hamel) Jones, and my two children, Cheryl and Scott.

Before we were married, I suggested to Sharlene that maybe I should chat with her three children, since she had already met mine. When it came time to talk further with her daughter, Laura, whom I had previously met in Italy, we arranged to meet at a local First Watch restaurant on a rainy day. I was already seated in a booth when Laura arrived, shaking the water off her raincoat. She sat down and immediately blurted out, "I think there is something you really need to know about my mother." I thought that our forthcoming marriage was in real trouble. Then, Laura continued with a smile on her face, "She always burns the rolls during a dinner party." I breathed a strong sigh of relief and we had a very nice lunch.

On December 1, 2006, we were married at a ceremony at the Royal Palm Yacht Club by Sharlene's cousin Brett Morin, a Baptist minister (Figure 2). We were thus able to become Peg Rogers' ninth successful matchmaking project. That is also why we tell folks we have an "arranged marriage." I also like to tell folks that "even a blind hog can find an acorn every now and then." Thankfully, Sharlene was my acorn. We lovingly

Fig. 2 Jim and Sharlene

share each other's conservative political views and moral/ethical values. We have been happily married ever since.

Sharlene and I also share similar views regarding race relations. In the military as well as in the civilian world, we have learned to judge others based upon their merits and character, not by their skin color. Further, our experience has shown that loyalty works both ways. Through the years many people of color have been loyal to us. In our lives we hope and pray that our loyalty to them has shown, especially when they needed it.

In the opening chapter I noted that because my parents both worked, my sister and I had been largely raised by Mary Jones, a Black woman from Arcadia. She truly was part of our family. After my sister and I left home, my mother continued to help her in numerous ways until Mary died. In the same way, Sharlene's children had also largely been raised by Marie Walker, a Black woman in Fort Myers. After Sharlene's family had grown, she employed another Black woman (Figure 3), Hazel Nerrow, to help her with housework and entertaining. Through the years Sharlene established long-lasting and warm relationships with both Marie and Hazel. Marie died several years ago, but Sharlene still considers Hazel part of our family. As Hazel has aged, Sharlene, on a continual basis, helps her in many ways, especially with Thanksgiving and Christmas dinners, and assists her with her finances and proper medications.

During my military career, I have worked with Black command sergeants major and first sergeants, as well as numerous Black and Latino officers, NCOs and soldiers. While there is a leadership distinction between commissioned officer and enlisted, our relationships were all based on mutual respect. Further, and especially in combat, I would not ask anything of any of them that I would not expect of myself. All performed very well and through the years, I have remained good friends with several.

Fig. 3 Hazel Nerrow

Yes, It Is Certainly Possible to Love Again

Marriage changed both of our lives. Before we married, Sharlene and I had our respective attorneys put together a prenuptial agreement, which in essence said whatever real property and financial assets that each brought into the marriage would remain separate. However, we agreed that we would share everyday living expenses. We did this to preclude inheritance issues that plague many previously married couples.

The first test of the agreement came when we had to decide where to live. My house was in North Fort Myers, hers in Fort Myers proper. We sought advice from a mutual friend, our county property appraiser, who suggested that for tax purposes, we sell my house and live in Sharlene's.

It took a while to sell my house, which turned out to be fortuitous. Once we were married, we began to spend our summers at Sharlene's condo in Banner Elk, North Carolina. A year or so after we were married, we got a call with bad news from a friend, Skip Mitchell, who checked on Sharlene's Fort Myers house. He said that when he walked around the house, water was flowing out the back door. When he went inside, he found that a water heater connection had failed and the house was flooded. After he turned the water off, he called us. We immediately returned to Fort Myers to find the house unlivable.

While the repairs were being made, we lived in my house in North Fort Myers. Sharlene took advantage of the remedial work to upgrade her kitchen and put in new flooring in various parts of the house. My house eventually sold later that year and the proceeds, according to terms of the prenuptial agreement, went into one of my personal accounts.

Sharlene and I continued to spend our summers in Banner Elk until the fall of 2017. Until that time, both Sharlene and I served on the board of the condo association and actively participated in events in the general area. We still maintain contact with the many friends we made in the North Carolina mountains.

In the fall of 2017, we made the decision to simplify our lives by downsizing into a continuing care facility. By this time, we were getting older and it was getting difficult to maintain both our mountain home and the one in Fort Myers. We had too much house and too much yard. We felt that we wanted to stay in the general Fort Myers area because that was where most of our friends were. We then visited all of the independent and assisted living facilities in the Fort Myers area. We put together a matrix of the various aspects of the places we visited and finally decided on an independent living duplex on the campus of Brookdale College Parkway, a large continuing care facility in Fort Myers. We sold the North Carolina condo in the fall of 2017 and the Fort Myers house during the summer of 2018, with the proceeds going into Sharlene's personal accounts.

With our move into Brookdale, our everyday routine changed very little. Although Brookdale has a wide range of activities available to residents, Sharlene and I took the advice of my daughter's friend's parents, who advised us that we should not get so involved with Brookdale activities that we lose touch with our longtime friends. Thus, we have not lost touch with our other friends. We continue to serve on the various boards of community organizations and remain members of the same social/political organizations with which we were previously affiliated.

Sharlene and I travel quite a bit with longtime friends and church members Pamela and John Noland. We have shown them West Point. We have visited California and New York City. In addition, we make an annual European trip together to thank the various Italian agencies that were involved in my rescue. We plan to continue to do these things as long as our health allows, albeit knowing that we have the Brookdale resources when they are needed.

In 2018, I began seeing a pulmonologist for an incipient cough. We tried a number of medications, but none seemed to work, so he ordered an MRI. The MRI showed that I had a spot on my left lung, so Dr. Chadha (Figure 4) ordered a biopsy. The biopsy discovered that I had a metastasized melanoma from a series of skin cancer treatments I had been receiving. My dermatologist had previously told me that I was a victim of the "blond, blue-eyed curse" and could expect continuous sun-induced problems with my skin. He was right on target. I am now seeing Dr. Anthony Fransway (Figure 5) every three months for removal of precancerous skin problems. But I digress.

Dr. Chadha referred me to Dr. Harwin (Figure 6), an oncologist whom he said had very good success with an immunology treatment for melanoma in the lungs. After a rigorous examination, Dr. Harwin initiated the immunology treatments. The treatments involved a monthly blood test and subsequent infusion of a cocktail tailored to the blood test. After a series of monthly infusions, an MRI showed that the spots on my lung had disappeared. I now see Dr. Harwin quarterly to confirm remission.

Thus, consistent with my philosophy of life, I believe that the good Lord still has something that I need to do. I have had many events in my years that were life-threatening and have thus far survived them all. This one, late in life, is no exception. I will do my very best to live up to my purpose for being, following my Pole Star.

As I write this, summer/fall of 2020, and winter of 2021, we at Brookdale are locked down due to the COVID-19 pandemic. Thus far, we have been spared, another indicator that hopefully, God has something else in store for me.

Fig. 5 Dr. Fransway and Jim

Fig. 4 Dr. Chadha

Fig. 6 Dr. Harwin

CHAPTER 12

Florida Veterans Hall of Fame Nomination

This chapter shows two of the more recent honors given me. The first is one of the greatest honors of my life: my nomination for and acceptance into the State of Florida Veterans Hall of Fame. The nomination package below was produced by fellow military officers, mainly retired Commander Doug Quelch, in the Lee Coast Chapter Military Officers Association of America. I was deeply honored by inclusion into the Hall of Fame with the Class of 2015. The induction ceremony took place at the state capital in Tallahassee in November 2015 led by Governor Rick Scott. With Sharlene, we were further honored that evening by a reception in the governor's mansion. The nomination package is a good summary of my adult life.

Sharlene and I were led to believe that the reception following the induction ceremony was for those recently inducted. We were wrong. When we got off the bus at the governor's mansion, we were surprised to join a huge crowd. We thought that surely not this many people were interested in the Florida Veterans Hall of Fame. We were right; it turned out that the induction ceremony coincided with the governor's birthday, so we joined a crowd of about 600 of the governor's closest friends, including Randy Henderson, the mayor of Fort Myers.

The second honor, which is shown later in this chapter, was the dedication of the State of Florida Military Officers of America Council of

Chapters Annual Convention Journal at the 2018 convention, hosted by the Lee Coast Chapter. Receiving these two honors, late in life, humble me in ways I find difficult to describe. I hope by their inclusion here, you will see a life of well-lived service; one that I am proud of but humbled by what God has given me.

Florida Veterans Hall of Fame

Nomination Package – 2015

JAMES LEE DOZIER – MAJOR GENERAL, U.S. ARMY (RETIRED)

Section 1. Florida Veterans Hall of Fame Nomination Form: Attached.

Section 2. Verification of Veteran's Status:

James Lee Dozier – Major General, U.S. Army (Retired)

(DD Form 214 Attached)

Section 3. Summary of Education and Training Accomplishments:

1949: Graduate, DeSoto County High School, Arcadia, Florida

1956: Graduate, United States Military Academy, West Point, BS Degree

1956: Graduate, U.S. Army Armor Officer Basic Course – 16 Weeks

1957: Graduate, U.S. Army Ranger Course, 8 Weeks, Authorized Ranger Tab

1957: Graduate, U.S. Army Airborne Course, 6 Weeks, Authorized Parachutist Badge

1962: Graduate, U.S. Army Armor Officer Advanced Course – 36 Weeks

1964: Graduate, University of Arizona, MS Degree in Aerospace Engineering

1968: Graduate, U.S. Army Command and General Staff College

1974: Graduate, U.S. Army War College

1978: Graduate, Defense Language Institute 24-Week Course in Italian

Section 4. Summary of Professional and Employment History:

Major Military Assignments

1950–1952 – Enlisted service with the Florida National Guard

1952–1956 – Cadet, United States Military Academy, West Point, New York

1956 – Commissioned 2nd Lt, Armor, United States Military Academy

1959–1960 – Troop Commander, G Troop, 2nd Armored Cavalry Regiment, Germany

1964 – MS Degree in Aerospace Engineering, University of Arizona

1964–1967 – Professor, Department of Mechanics, United States Military Academy
1967–1968 – Army CGSC (Command and General Staff College), Fort
Leavenworth
1968–1969 – S-3 (Operations) 11th Armored Cavalry Regiment, Vietnam
1969–1971 – DCSOPS (Deputy Chief of Staff, Operations), Pentagon
1971–1973 – Squadron Commander, 1st Squadron, 1st Cavalry, 1st Armored Division,
Germany
1973–1974 – United States Army War College
1973–1976 – Staff, Office of Assistant Secretary of the Army for Research and
Development and Assistant Secretary of the Army for Financial Management,
Pentagon
1976–1978 – Brigade Commander, 2nd Brigade, 2nd Armored Division, Fort Hood,
Texas
1978–1979 – Chief of Staff, 2nd Armored Division, Fort Hood, Texas
1979–1980 – Chief of Staff, III Corps, Fort Hood, Texas
1980–1982 – Assistant Chief of Staff, Administration & Logistics, Allied Land
Forces Southern Europe, Verona, Italy
1982–1983 – Deputy Commander, U.S. Army Armor Center, Fort Knox, Kentucky
1983–1985 – Deputy Commanding General, III Corps, Fort Hood, Texas
1985 – Retired from Military Service

Post-Military Business Career in Florida

1985–2004:
Owner, JCS Group – An anti-terrorism, agricultural and leadership consulting
organization
Former President – Golden Groves Division of American Agronomics
Former Assistant to the Publisher – Sun Coast Media Group
Former General Manager, David C. Brown Farms
Owner, JCS Citrus and JCS Nursery (now inactive)

Professional Business Associations

Florida Citrus Mutual – Member
Southwest Florida Croton Society – Member with son
Southwest Florida Water Management District Agriculture Advisory Committee –
Former Member
IFIS Citrus Advisory committee – Past President
Gulf Citrus Growers Governmental Affairs Committee – Former Member

Peace River Valley Citrus Growers Association – Former Member
Florida Nurserymen and Growers Association – Member
Gulf Citrus Exposition Advisory Council – Past Member
2004–Present: Retired

Section 5. Summary of Nominee's Advocacy on behalf of Veterans:

The following is a list of the Veterans Organizations in which General Dozier has been involved:

Korean War Veterans Association – Member
The United States Armor Association – Member
The Military Order of the World Wars – Member
The American Legion – Member
The Veterans of Foreign Wars – Member
The Association of the U.S. Army – Member
The Air Force Association – Member
West Point Society of Naples – Member
Disabled Veterans Insurance Careers – Member
Caloosa Chapter, Sons of the American Revolution – Member
Florida Commission on Veterans Affairs – Former Member
Lee Coast Chapter, Military Officers of America Association – Board Member

The above list shows the active involvement of General Dozier in veterans' organizations. However, his involvement is more extensive than just belonging to an organization. He is in demand as a speaker at Veterans Day ceremonies and for other functions, and he participates in Veterans in the Classroom, reaching out to students in Lee County schools. He speaks often to community organizations about veterans affairs. Through his financial support and active involvement, he has been instrumental in working to set up veterans scholarships at Hodges University.

As a Board member of the Lee Coast Chapter, Military Officers of America Association, he has championed major donations to the Wounded Warriors of South Florida, the Fisher Houses at the James A. Haley, Tampa FL. and Bay Pines, St. Petersburg FL VA Hospitals and the Lee Memorial Hospital Military Support Program. He was active as a former member of the Florida Commission on Veterans Affairs. In looking to future veterans, General Dozier was the Chairman of former Congressman Connie Mack's Service Academy Nominating Committee. Through his financial support, each year he awards the prestigious

Major General James L. Dozier Award to the outstanding cadet, selected from the more than 5,200 students enrolled in the JROTC programs at the 14 Lee County high schools.

As a veteran, General Dozier is also an Adjunct Professor at the USAF Special Operations School and a former Board member of the Florida Air Academy.

Section 6. Summary of Nominee's Civic Activities and Contributions

Wesley Memorial Methodist Church – Lay Reader
Thomas A. Edison Congregational Church – Member
Business People United for Political Activity – President
Downtown Rotary Club – Member
Congressman Connie Mack's Service Academy Nominating Committee – Former Chairman
Southwest Florida Community Foundation – Member
Southwest Council Boy Scouts of America – Former Executive Board Member
Florida Commission on Veterans Affairs – Former Member
Goodwill Life Academy – Former Board Member
American Heart Association – Past Chairman, Fort Myers Heart Walk
Florida International Air Show – Past President
North Fort Myers Rotary Club – Former Member (transferred to Downtown Rotary Club)
Lee District Schools Superintendent Search Committee, 1997 – Chairman
Good Wheels – Board Member, Past Chairman
Seminole Electric Cooperative Incorporated – Board Member
Lee County Electric Cooperative – Board Secretary, Member of Executive Committee
Tampa Bay Area Council on Foreign Relations – Former Member

The above summary is extensive; however, General Dozier does not just belong to organizations. He is an active participant in all the organizations and community service projects to which he belongs. His status as a former General officer in the U.S. armed services allows his voice to be heard, and with his extensive experience, he is instrumental in the successful completion of community projects.

Section 7. List any awards or honors:

Awarded the **Silver Star** for heroism and the **Purple Heart** for wounds received in combat in Vietnam. Other military personal awards include the **Legion of Merit**, the **Bronze Star** with two Oak Leaf Clusters and Combat "V", the **Meritorious Service Medal** with one Oak Leaf Cluster, the **Air Medal** with one Oak Leaf Cluster, the **Army Commendation Medal** with one Oak Leaf Cluster, and the **Army Good Conduct Medal**. He also holds the **Ranger Tab** and the **Parachutist Badge**.

As a Brigadier General, in 1981, General Dozier was kidnapped from his apartment in Verona, Italy by an Italian Red Brigades terrorist cell and held for 42 days. A bloodless assault by a special operations unit of the Italian police released him from his captors. Upon release, he was congratulated by President Reagan. As a result of his kidnapping, he currently serves as an anti-terrorism consultant to various government and private agencies.

Appointed by Governor Jeb Bush as one of Florida's 27 Electors in the 2004 Presidential Election.

Section 8. Written Narrative:

General Jim Dozier is a bona fide American hero. This is not only from his service in Vietnam, where he was wounded and awarded the Silver Star for heroism, but also from his conduct while being held captive by a terrorist organization in Italy. Despite his 35 years of military service with the U.S. Army and NATO, in the United States, Europe and Asia, he has never forgotten his Florida roots. Born in Arcadia, on graduating from high school and before his active military service, he enlisted in the Florida National Guard, where he served for two years. It was there that his officer-like qualities were recognized and he was selected to the prestigious United States Military Academy at West Point.

On retirement from active military service, he came back to Florida and was involved in agribusiness for 20 more years before retiring again in 2004. During that 20-year period and since, he has been actively involved in community groups and veterans' organizations, making his mark as a "can-do" person. The following list summarizes his lifetime:

Thirty-five years successful military leadership and management experience in both command and staff positions at all levels of authority from platoon to the NATO coalition.

Twenty-plus years successful leadership and management experience in the private sector (as President/CEO, General Manager, Owner,

Board Member, and Board Chairman) with large and small business organizations.

Fifty-plus years experience successfully interfacing and working with city, county, state, federal and international government agencies and elected/appointed officials.

Seventeen years on-the-job experience as a trustee of the Lee County Electric Cooperative. His well-developed and applied leadership, management and business skills, plus experience with the dynamics of government and private organizations and businesses have made him a proven citizen. Without doubt, General Dozier has made significant contributions to the state of Florida in veterans, civic, business and public service pursuits. He has served tirelessly in his efforts for the community and the state and is well deserving of the honor to be inducted into the Florida Veterans Hall of Fame.

* * *

The article below was printed in the Lee Coast MOAA newsletter after his selection for the Class of 2015 Florida Veterans Hall of Fame:

Major General Jim Dozier Selected for Florida Veterans Hall of Fame

Our own Major General Jim Dozier was recently selected for induction with four others into the Florida Veterans Hall of Fame. After an extensive nomination process by our Chapter, Jim was selected for the Class of 2015. He will be honored at a dinner with Governor Scott in Tallahassee later this year.

General Dozier is a bona fide American hero. This is not only from his service in Vietnam, where he was wounded and awarded the Silver Star for heroism, but also from his conduct while being held captive by a terrorist organization in Italy. As a Brigadier General, in 1981, General Dozier was kidnapped from his apartment in Verona, Italy by an Italian Red Brigades terrorist cell and held for 42 days. A bloodless assault by a special operations unit of the Italian police released him from his captors. Upon release, he was congratulated by President Reagan. As a result of his kidnapping, he serves as an anti-terrorism consultant to various government and private agencies.

During his 35 years of military service with the U.S. Army and NATO, in the United States, Europe and Asia, his successful military leadership and management experience was demonstrated in both command and staff positions at all levels of authority. During all this time, he never forgot his Florida roots. Born in Arcadia, on graduating from high school and before his active military service, he enlisted in the Florida National Guard, where he served for two years. It was there that his officer-like qualities were recognized and he was selected to the prestigious United States Military Academy at West Point. Little known is that Jim holds an MS Degree in Aerospace Engineering, later obtained from the University of Arizona, and for three years he was a Professor in the Department of Mechanics at the United States Military Academy.

On retirement from active military service, he came back to Florida and was involved in agribusiness for 20 more years before retiring again in 2004. During that 20-year period and since, he has been actively involved in community groups and veterans organizations, making his mark as a "can-do" person. We are honored to have him as a Chapter member and we hope many of our members will make the trip to Tallahassee with Jim and Sharlene for his induction.

* * *

This Convention Journal Is Dedicated to:

MAJOR GENERAL JAMES L. DOZIER, USA (Ret)

This Florida Council of Chapters 40th annual convention Journal is dedicated to Major General James Dozier of Lee Coast Chapter. After a lengthy and extensive nomination process by Lee Coast Chapter in 2015,

General Dozier was selected with four others to the Florida Veterans Hall of Fame. As a member of the Class of 2015, he was honored during his induction and later at a dinner with Governor Scott in Tallahassee.

General Dozier is a bona fide American hero. This is not only from his service in Vietnam, where he was wounded and awarded the Silver Star for heroism, but also from his conduct while being held captive by a terrorist organization in Italy. As a Brigadier General in 1981, General Dozier was kidnapped from his apartment in Verona, Italy by an Italian Red Brigades terrorist cell and held for 42 days. A bloodless assault by a special operations unit of the Italian police released him from his captors. Upon release, he was congratulated by President Reagan. As a result of this experience, he serves as an anti-terrorism consultant to various government and private agencies. Jim also holds the Army Distinguished Service medal and also was awarded a number of other combat-related medals.

During his 35 years of military service with the U.S. Army and NATO, in the United States, Europe, and Asia, his successful military leadership and management experience was demonstrated in both command and staff positions at all levels. During all this time, he never forgot his Florida roots. Born in Arcadia and on graduating from high school, he enlisted in the Florida National Guard where he served for two years. It was there that his officer-like qualities were recognized and he was selected for the United States Military Academy at West Point. As a West Point graduate, little known is that Jim also holds an MS Degree in Aerospace Engineering, later obtained from the University of Arizona. For three years he was a professor in the Department of Mechanics at the United States Military Academy.

On retirement from active military service, he came back to Florida and was involved in agribusiness for 20 more years before retiring again in 2004. During that 20-year period and the 14 years since, Jim has been actively involved in community groups and veterans organizations, making his mark as a "can do" person. Lee Coast Chapter is honored to have him as a Chapter member, while he still remains active in southwest Florida community affairs.

What Friends Do!

Some friends of mine from the military put together this cartoon as a reminder of my kidnapping:

Postscript

To stay in contact with those who rescued me and who supported my family during our kidnapping experience, we have made a special effort to return to Italy, as frequently as possible. Each time we go back, we thank our rescuers once again for their efforts on our behalf. The Dozier family now tries to return on an annual schedule. We have had the good fortune to be most ably assisted in making these trips because of several special friends in Italy.

Rome

In Rome, about 15 years after I was res-cued, I was contacted by an exceptional lady, Raffaella Cortese de Bosis. At the time of my kidnapping, she was on the staff with *NBC News* in Rome. She was now with RAI Italian State Television and asked me to do a special program for her station on the kidnapping. I readily agreed. That started a friendship that exists to this day, not only with Raffaella, but also with her father, Ambassador Cortese, a gifted diplomat, who was a member of Italian Intelligence and liaison officer with the British 8th Army, including the 8th Indian Division, during WWII (Figure 1).

Fig. 1 Ambassador Alessandro Cortese de Bosis

Over time, Raffaella (Figure 2) arranged for us to meet the members of the kidnapping rescue team, led by Edoardo Perna, deputy commander of NOCS. In addition, he intro-duced us to Inspector Improta, head of the anti-terrorism unit of UCIGOS, and his fam-ily, the various other NOCS commanders, and members of the Italian and city of Rome gov-ernments. She also arranged meetings with the chiefs of Italian National Police Prefect Anto-nio Manganelli and Prefect Franco Gabrielli. On the 30th anniversary of my rescue, we had

Fig. 2 Raffaella Cortese de Bosis

a special dinner at a local restaurant where Edoardo Perna announced the publication of his book about the kidnapping. I thanked each member of the rescue team and presented them with medallions commemorating the 30th anniversary of their accomplishment. On another trip to the NOCS headquarters and training camp, the NOCS honored me with a celebration of my birthday.

Several years ago, Raffaella was instrumental in arranging for me to help an Italian farmer, Fabio Dalmonte, who had found the WWII dog tags of Mack Tays, an American soldier who

Fig. 3 Raffaella and Jim

had died in northern Italy. He wanted to return them to the Tays family. Since I was scheduled to do some security consulting work about that time in nearby Vicenza, I readily agreed. Accompanied by my host at the security conference in Vicenza, we met Fabio and Raffaella at an autostrada interchange. He then led us to his farmhouse. We had an emotional ceremony on the patio of Fabio's house, during which time the dog tags were entrusted to my care. American and Italian flags were displayed and both countries' national anthems were played.

Raffaella was present and translated the proclamations from the various U.S. and Italian government agencies, which the farmer and I read. Fabio then took us on a four-wheel drive ride and hike through the northern Italian mountains to show us where the dog tags and soldier's remains were found. The soldier's remains were found at the bottom of a pretty steep hill. As we approached the spot, Fabio said that the dog tags were found farther up the hill, but for us to wait while he went up the hill to mark the spot. When he reached the spot, he unfurled a large American flag. During the war, Fabio's family had been members of the Italian Resistance. They sincerely thanked me for the help we Americans gave the Resistance in Italy.

Shortly thereafter, Raffaella made arrangements with the city of Florence, Alabama, for us to turn over Mack Tays' dog tags to his sole surviving sister on Veterans Day in 2015. In order for Raffaella to participate in the veterans ceremony in Florence, we arranged for her to fly from Rome to Miami, where we picked her up (Figure 3). We then drove to Florence. The very emotional turnover ceremony was held before a large crowd in the Florence Veterans Park.

Northern Italy

In northern Italy, especially in Verona, we have been ably assisted by U.S. Army Colonel (Ret) Mario Gargiulo and his wife, Norma (Figure 4). Mario and Norma, now deceased, were old friends with whom we had served at HQ LANDSOUTH (Land Component of the Southern Command of NATO) from 1980-82. Mario had attended the Italian Air Force Academy, and since he spoke both fluent Italian and English, he had been serving as an aide to Italian General Santini, CINC of LANDSOUTH. General

Fig. 4 Mario and Norma

Santini had very graciously allowed Mario to accompany Judy and me on our trip back to the U.S., immediately after my rescue.

Norma Gargiulo is a New York City native, raised in an Italian family. She also speaks both fluent English and Italian. As previously mentioned, she acted as our interpreter during the trial of my kidnappers. At our request, on the 30th anniversary of my rescue, Norma arranged a special dinner in Verona for those who assisted my family and who helped prosecute the kidnappers. Sharlene was with me for the occasion. The invitees included former members of the LANDSOUTH staff, as well as special friends, plus Doctor Papalia, who had prosecuted the kidnappers. The multi-course dinner was held at a special, upscale restaurant that was closed to accommodate the occasion. The chef specialized in centuries-old Italian recipes.

Fig. 5 Italy presentations

The first course of the dinner consisted of a compote filled with a black substance topped by a white substance. It looked a little strange, so Sharlene was dubious about tasting it. It turned out to be squid ink topped by cream. It was a little salty, but absolutely delicious. The next course was fried sardines, another delicacy. The courses that followed were more standard, in that they were foods we had previously eaten in Italy.

After dinner, we all made speeches and exchanged gifts (Figure 5). General Donati, a former chief of staff, LANDSOUTH, gave an eloquent talk, as did Dr. Papalia. Thanks to Norma's very thoughtful and diligent work, it was a truly memorable evening.

Mario, Norma and Raffaella, working with local law enforcement agencies, also made it possible for us to visit the Padova apartment in which I was held. In addition, we have gotten to know their son Julian, a superb, dynamic concert pianist. We have had the privilege of hosting him at one of his concerts in North Carolina.

Fort Myers Friends Who Travel With Us

For the past 10 years, our special Fort Myers friends, Pamela and John Noland (Figure 6), have accompanied us on our trips to Italy and various other parts of Europe. In addition to traveling in Italy and getting to know our Italian friends, we have visited Paris, Omaha Beach, Bastogne and Switzerland. We usually rent a car at the arrival airport in Europe and turn it in at the departure airport.

Fig. 6 Pam and John Noland

Together, we have become fond of Montalcino, a little hilltop town in Tuscany in the Brunello wine region, so on each trip, we usually plan to spend as much time there as possible. Each fall, Montalcino holds its harvest festival. They call it, "The Thrush Festival." The town is divided up into quarters, each with its own king and queen, special colors, marching songs and archers. They dress in medieval costumes. On the final Sunday, there is an archery contest with long bows. At 42 meters, they are able to get shot patterns the size of a dinner plate. Each year, we look forward to our annual trip to Europe. We plan to continue these trips as long as we are able.

Epilogue

Major General James Lee
Dozier, U.S. Army (Ret)

As I pointed out in the previous chapters, I did not grow up with a desire to be a military or a community leader. God took care of that. As I put my life in perspective, God made it possible for me to do both by providing me with great parents, a strong, supportive family, exceptional mentors and leaders, plus good friends. I have done the best I can to have lived up to their expectations.

All of those who touched my life, both good and bad, helped me develop my Pole Star. They provided principles that guided me toward a life of service, both to our great nation and to our community. Above all else, they inculcated in me that strong leadership is everything, without it, our free society just won't tick. With it, America provides a beacon of freedom and opportunity for those who are less fortunate. I firmly believe in American exceptionalism; thus, I pray every day for those leaders who are making decisions on behalf of our country, so that our nation heads in the direction that God would have it go, as a leader of the free world. It has been my privilege to have been part of that process. I close with words taken from the third verse of the West Point Alma Mater:

And when our work is done, our course on earth is run,
may it be said 'well done; be thou at peace.'

MAY GOD CONTINUE TO BLESS AMERICA

Appendix A

DEPARTMENT OF THE ARMY
HEADQUARTERS, II FIELD FORCE VIETNAM
APO San Francisco 96266

GENERAL ORDERS
NUMBER 1965

20 May 1970

AWARD OF THE SILVER STAR

1. TC 439. The following AWARD is announced.

DOZIER, JAMES L 261-42-4071 MAJOR ARMOR United States Army 11TH ARMORED CAVALRY
REGIMENT APO 96257
Awarded: Silver Star
Date of service: 15 April 1970
Theater: Republic of Vietnam
Reason: Major Dozier distinguished himself by gallantry in action while engaged in
military operations involving conflict with an armed hostile force on
15 April 1970 while serving as the S-3, 11th Armored Cavalry Regiment, in the
Republic of Vietnam. On this date Major Dozier was flying in his light observation helicopter, observing and monitoring an engagement between Troop C and
an enemy force in bunkers. He noted that one platoon became separated from
the remainder of the troop in the dense jungle, thus dangerously exposing its
flank to a well protected, heavily armed enemy force located in an adjacent
bunker complex. Major Dozier tried to establish contact with the commander
on the ground, but because of the intensity of the engagement below he was
unable to do so. Major Dozier, realizing the seriousness of the situation,
ordered the pilot of his observation helicopter to fly low over the enemy position
so that his door gunner and pilot could engage them with machine gun fire.
After making several firing passes and still unable to make radio contact with
the platoon, or to get his instructions relayed to the platoon by the troop
commander, he ordered his pilot to land in a small and dangerously exposed
clearing in the jungle near the disoriented platoon. Upon landing, Major
Dozier, exposing himself to enemy fire, immediately proceeded to the platoon's
position. Intense enemy antitank fire had damaged two vehicles and seriously
wounded several crew members, thus contributing to further disorganization of
the platoon. After conferring with the platoon leader, he reorganized the force
and led the small force in an attack against the enemy positions. After closing
on the enemy, Major Dozier continued to direct the fire of the small force
until the enemy position had been overrun and then led a sweep of the battle
area to clear it of remaining enemy. Only after the wounded had been evacuated and
the platoon had rejoined the remainder of the troop, did Major Dozier depart the
battle area. Major Dozier's actions were in keeping with the highest traditions
of the military service and reflect great credit upon himself, his unit and the
United States Army.
Authority: By direction of the President under the provisions of the Act of Congress,
approved 9 July 1918.

FOR THE COMMANDER:

OFFICIAL:

E. THOMAS
Colonel, AGC
Adjutant General

F. J. ROBERTS
Brigadier General, GS
Chief of Staff

DISTRIBUTION:
5-Indiv
5-UPO, 11th Armored Cavalry Regiment, APO 96257
5-AVFB-IO
6-AVFB-AGD
2-CO, Unit concerned
2-AVFBA
2-AVFB-A
1-CG, USARV, APO 96375

SPECIAL DISTRIBUTION:
1-TAGO, DA, ATTN: AGPF-P, Wash, D. C. — 20315
(Off Official Pers Rec File)

Silver Star Citation

Appendix B

THE UNITED STATES OF AMERICA

TO ALL WHO SHALL SEE THESE PRESENTS, GREETING:

THIS IS TO CERTIFY THAT
THE PRESIDENT OF THE UNITED STATES OF AMERICA
AUTHORIZED BY ACT OF CONGRESS JULY 9, 1918
HAS AWARDED

THE SILVER STAR

TO

MAJOR JAMES L. DOZIER, 261-42-4071, ARMOR
UNITED STATES ARMY

FOR

GALLANTRY IN ACTION

IN THE REPUBLIC OF VIETNAM ON 15 APRIL 1969

GIVEN UNDER MY HAND IN THE CITY OF WASHINGTON
THIS   19TH   DAY OF   MAY   1970

MICHAEL S. DAVISON
Lieutenant General, USA

SECRETARY OF THE ARMY

Silver Star Medal

Appendix C

THE UNITED STATES OF AMERICA

TO ALL WHO SHALL SEE THESE PRESENTS, GREETING:

THIS IS TO CERTIFY THAT
THE PRESIDENT OF THE UNITED STATES OF AMERICA
AUTHORIZED BY EXECUTIVE ORDER, FEBRUARY 4, 1944
HAS AWARDED

THE BRONZE STAR MEDAL
WITH "V" DEVICE
(FIRST OAK LEAF CLUSTER)

TO

MAJOR JAMES L. DOZIER, 261-42-4071, ARMOR
UNITED STATES ARMY

FOR

HEROISM IN GROUND COMBAT

IN THE REPUBLIC OF VIETNAM ON 19 APRIL 1969

GIVEN UNDER MY HAND IN THE CITY OF WASHINGTON
THIS   2D   DAY OF   NOVEMBER   19 69

JULIAN J. EWELL
Lieutenant General, USA

STANLEY R. RESOR
SECRETARY OF THE ARMY

Bronze Star Medal

Finding My Pole Star Study Guide

By Douglas B. Quelch, Commander, U.S. Navy (Ret)

1. How would you describe a Pole Star; not just in terms of navigation at sea or on land, but as a guiding principle in your life?

2. Do you have memories as a child growing up that played a part in forming the person you are today? What were some of the things you did, either by yourself or with a young group of friends?

3. General Dozier developed discipline in his life, not only through his parents and concerned teachers, but also through experiences at West Point and a career in the military. Can you describe the factors in your life that brought you to maturity?

4. As a boy growing up, General Dozier was partially raised by a Black woman who became part of his family. Early on he developed a sense of racial equality that served him well in his military career. In retirement he and his wife Sharlene are helping to support a Black woman who helped raise Sharlene's children. What experiences in your life have brought you understanding and concern for different cultures and races?

5. Religion has always been very important to General Dozier. How has religion or another ethical code played a role in shaping the type of person you have become?

6. Wars are unpleasant and are the ultimate failures of diplomacy. General Dozier is a decorated American hero who was injured in battle in Vietnam. He has certain views on the conduct of the Vietnam war. Has your opinion of war changed after reading of General Dozier's experiences? If so, how?

7. In Vietnam, General Dozier met a Vietnamese Army Ranger Battalion commander who had a sign hung in his mess hall that said: *Those who have never lost it and have never had to fight to regain it, can never know the true meaning of the word Freedom.* What does "Freedom" mean to you, and what would you do if you lost it?

8. A terrifying yet defining moment in General Dozier's life was his kidnapping by the Italian terrorist group, the Red Brigades. Like many released prisoners of war, the experience was a hermetic one, with him sealed off from the outside world. Have you ever had an experience that helps you to empathize with General Dozier's kidnapping and isolation?

9. General Dozier has a master's degree in aeronautical engineering and taught in the Department of Mechanics at West Point. His post-military career was in agriculture. Have you ever had such a drastic change in occupations? If so, what factors in your own life led to your decision for making such a change?

10. After promotion to general officer, General Dozier attended a course at the Center for Creative Leadership that allowed attendees to give each other a look at themselves through the eyes of others. How did this exercise help General Dozier in his leadership role? Would you welcome such an exercise within your own group? Why or why not?

11. At the American Academy of Achievement, General Dozier was asked what motivated him in his life. What has motivated you?

12. Giving back to the community has been important to General Dozier. How have you given back to your town or city?

Acknowledgments

Commander, US Navy (Ret) Doug Quelch, a leader in our Southwest Florida retired military community, who served as editor, technical advisor and cheerleader. Without Doug's wizardry with a computer and his command of the English language (especially grammar, punctuation and spelling), this story would have never seen the light of day. Doug was also the driver behind my admission to the Florida Veterans Hall of Fame. I appreciate his many suggestions and I will be forever grateful for his help and friendship.

Colonel, US Army (Ret) Mario Gargiulo and his wife Norma, friends who reside in Verona, Italy, and who greatly assisted my family during my kidnapping and who also serve as our points of contact for our trips to northern Italy. Mario kept a diary of our post-kidnapping trip to the United States, which he has generously shared for the writing of this story. Norma, now deceased, served as the translator for Judy and me during the trial of the kidnappers.

Joan (Dozier) Rossano, my dear sister, now deceased, who provided companionship for Judy during her visit to Italy right after my kidnapping. Joan was also an ardent collector of newspaper clippings associated with the kidnapping which were of considerable help in putting this story together. She also served as quality control for stories of events during our younger years.

Raffaella Cortese de Bosis, our dear friend in Rome, whose efforts have provided access to key figures in Italy who played a role in my kidnapping and who contributed to a better understanding of associated events. She continues to keep us in contact with all of our Italian friends and makes our trips to Rome very special. She has been instrumental in researching stories of fallen Italian American soldiers and other soldiers who contributed to the liberation of Italy during WWII. During WWII, Raffaella's father, Ambassador Cortese de Bosis, a recently retired member of the Italian Department of State, was a member of the resistance.

Glee Duff, a friend in Fort Myers, with whom I served on many boards, for his insistence that I write this story.

My wife, Sharlene, who patiently read my work, made suggestions for additions and deletions, and who kept my nose to the grindstone.

My many friends, in and out of the military, who played influential roles in helping a small-town boy develop a Pole Star that served him well during his military and community service.

For the readers, all proceeds derived from the sale of this book will go into the Southwest Florida Community Foundation, a 501(c)(3) foundation, to be used to support the General James L. Dozier JROTC Support Fund, used to support and augment the 16 high school Junior Reserve Officer Training Corps (JROTC) units in the Lee County, Florida schools. Of note, the Lee County JROTC program, with over 8,000 cadets, is the largest in the nation.

Patton Reunions

For more than 40 years, those of us who served with General Patton have been holding what we call the annual Patton Reunion. We usually gather at the Patton farm (Green Meadows Farm) north of Boston. On several occasions, for old time's sake, our reunion has been held elsewhere, such as at Fort Hood, Texas, but usually each October, we trek up to the farm. George has now passed away and his original house and property have been donated to a local college, but his wife, Joanne, still lives on nearby property. There is also a convenient guest house on the farm property that Joanne makes available to us. She is an inspiration to all and dedicated to all who have served in our military, but especially to those who have served with her husband.

The reunions are an outgrowth of weekends spent together on trips to various parts of Texas that many of us, mostly colonels in the 2AD, would take as a group with our wives. General and Mrs. Patton had fostered teamwork and we furthered it with our weekends. At times we would invite those at Fort Hood who had served with him in other assignments.

After we all retired, we decided to continue getting together as an annual event. While he was still alive, we also decided to invite both George and Joanne Patton to join us, hence the name Patton Reunion. After his passing, we continue inviting Joanne to be with us to help celebrate all our memories.

Glossary

1st ID – First Infantry Division
2ACR – 2nd Armored Cavalry Regiment
5ATAF – 5th Allied Tactical Air Force
AAA – Anti-Aircraft Artillery
AAAC – American Academy of Achievement Conference
AC – Assistant Commandant
ADC – Assistant Division Commander
AFB – Air Force Base
AFSOUTH – Allied Forces Southern Europe
AG – Adjutant General
AO – Area of Operations
ANSA – Italian News Agency
ARVN – Army of the Republic of South Vietnam
ASA FM – Assistant Secretary of the Army, Financial Management
ASA R & D – Assistant Secretary of the Army, Research and Development
BCSM – Brigade Command Sergeant Major
BENELUX – Belgium, Netherlands and Luxemburg
BOQ – Bachelor Officer Quarters
Brief – Briefing
BUPAC – Business people United for Political Action Committee
C/S – Chief of Staff
CB Radio – Citizens Band Radio
CCL – Center for Creative Leadership
CEO – Chief Executive Officer
CG – Commanding General
CGSC – Command & General Staff College
CIA – Central Intelligence Agency
CID – Criminal Investigation Division
CINC – Commander in Chief
CO – Commanding Officer
Corps – Multi-division military organization

CP – Command Post
CSM – Command Sargent Major
DAPR – Department of the Army Program Review
DCC – Deputy Corps Commander
DCG – Deputy Commanding General
DCSOPS – Deputy Chief of Staff Operations
DIA – Defense Intelligence Agency
DIT – Dynamics of International Terrorism
DLI – Defense Language Institute
DOD – Department of Defense
Dong Ngai – VC Regiment
DRS Tests – Division Restructuring Study Tests
DRS – Division Restructuring Study
FAC – Forward Air Controller
FBI – Federal Bureau of Investigation
FORSCOM – Forces Command
FSCW – Florida State College for Women
FSU – Florida State University
GOMO – General Officer Management Office
GWU – George Washington University
Ho Chi Minh Trail – NVA supply line through Laos
HQ USARV – Headquarters US Army Viet Nam
HQ – Headquarters
ID – Infantry Division
ID Cards – Identification Cards
IFAS – Institute For Agricultural Sciences
IG – Inspector General
II Field Force – 2nd Field Force (Corps)
III Corps – 3rd United States Army Corps
ILS – Instrument Landing System
IPR – In Progress Review
JCS – Joint Chiefs of Staff
JROTC – Junior ROTC (High School Level)
JSOC – Joint Special Operations Command

JSOU – Joint Special Operations University

Kaserne – German for military installation

KIA – Killed in Action

KP – Kitchen Police

LANDSOUTH – Land component of the Southern Command of NATO

LCEC – Lee County Electric Cooperative

LOH – Light Observation Helicopter

MHC – Mars Hill College

MIT – Massachusetts Institute of Technology

NATO – North Atlantic Treaty Organization

NCO – Non-commissioned Officer (Corporals and Sergeants)

NJ – New Jersey

NOCS – Nucleo Operativo Centrale di Sicurezza – Italian National Police Hostage Rescue Team

NVA – North Vietnamese Army

NY – New York

OP – Observation Post

PAO – Public Affairs Officer

PBAC – Program and Budget Advisory Committee

POC – Point of Contact

POW – Prisoner of War

R & R – Rest and Relaxation

RAF – Red Army Faction

Recon – Reconnaissance

Red Brigades – Italian Left-Wing Terrorist Organization

REFORGER – REenFORcement of units in GERmany

ROTC – Reserve Officer Training Corps (College Level)

RPG – Rocket Propelled Grenade

RVN – Republic of South Vietnam

SAM – Surface to Air Missile

SAT – Scholastic Aptitude Test

SCMG – Sun Coast Media Group

SERE – Survive, Evade, Resist, Escape

SETAF – Southern European Task Force
TACAIR – Tactical Aircraft
TOC – Tactical Operations Center
U of A – University of Arizona
U of F – University of Florida
USAFA – United States Air Force Academy
USAF – United States Air Force
USAFE – United States Air Force Europe
USAREUR – United States Army, Europe
USARV – United States Army, Vietnam
USAWC – United States Army War College
UCIGOS – Italian civilian intelligence
USEUCOM – United States European Command
USMAPS – United States Military Academy Prep School
USMA – United States Military Academy
USMC – United States Marine Corps
USNA – United States Naval Academy
VC – Viet Cong
WWII – World War 2
XO – Executive Officer

STAFF OFFICERS

C/S – Chief of Staff
S–1 – Adjutant (Chief Administrative Officer)
S–2 – Intelligence Officer
S–3 – Operations and Training Officer
S–4 – Supply Officer

ARMY RANKS

CWO – Chief Warrant Officer
2LT – 2nd Lieutenant
1LT – 1st Lieutenant
CPT – Captain
MAJ – Major

LTC – Lieutenant Colonel
COL – Colonel
BG – Brigadier General
MG – Major General
LTG – Lieutenant General
GEN – Full General

USMA Terms

Plebe – Freshman at West Point
Yearling – Sophomore at West Point
Cow – Junior at West Point
Firstie – Senior at West Point
Goats – Slower learning cadets
Hives – Smarter cadets

Index

KIDNAPPERS

ETERNAL PRAYER

Dear Lord

Be thou a bright flame before me

Be thou a guiding star above me

Be thou a smooth path beneath me

Be thou a kindly shepherd behind me

Today and ever more.

Amen.

R & R

***

Recommended Reading

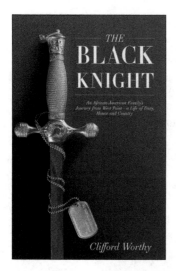

The Black Knight
by Clifford Worthy

Clifford Worthy, the great grandson of slaves, was one of the few African-American men of his generation who was accepted and excelled as a Black Knight of the Hudson, a traditional nickname for West Point cadets. Worthy describes his journey to West Point, the many challenges he overcame both in his family and in the U.S. Army, including service in the front lines of Vietnam.

Love, Loss and Endurance
by Bill Tammeus

Two decades after the terrorist attacks on 9/11, America still is reeling from lingering trauma. Award-winning journalist Bill Tammeus was among those who suffered the personal loss of a relative that day. In this inspiring and hopeful book, Tammeus takes us to the heart of that gripping drama. He helps us to understand the many sources of religious extremism — and what can be done to stop it.

Find these books on Amazon.com, BarnesandNoble.com, Walmart.com, AbeBooks.com and other retailers. eBook formats available.

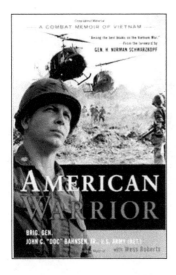

American Warrior:
A Combat Memoir of Vietnam

by John C. "Doc" Bahnsen, Jr. and
Wess Roberts

One of America's most decorated soldiers in the Vietnam War. The ultimate warrior who engaged the enemy from nearly every type of aircraft and armored vehicle in the Army's inventory. An expert strategist who developed military tactics later adopted as doctrine. Doc Bahnsen gives a full account of his astonishing war record.

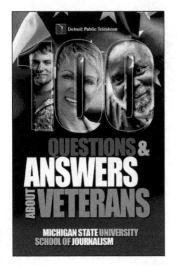

100 Questions and Answers about Veterans

by the Michigan State University
School of Journalism

This simple, introductory guide for civilians answers 100 basic questions about veterans. It has answers about military training, culture, families and structure. It talks about veterans' benefits, employment, contributions and challenges. This guide is for people in businesses, schools, government, law enforcement, human resources who need a starting point in learning about veterans.

CPSIA information can be obtained
at www.ICGtesting.com
Printed in the USA
BVHW051412210921
617190BV00002B/97